D1337107

IRENE ZEMPI AND IMRAN AWAN

ISLAMOPHOBIA

Lived experiences of online and offline
victimisation

POLICY PRESS SHORTS RESEARCH

First published in Great Britain in 2016 by

Policy Press
University of Bristol
1-9 Old Park Hill
Bristol
BS2 8BB
UK
t: +44 (0)117 954 5940
pp-info@bristol.ac.uk
www.policypress.co.uk

North America office:
Policy Press
c/o The University of Chicago Press
1427 East 60th Street
Chicago, IL 60637, USA
t: +1 773 702 7700
f: +1 773 702 9756
sales@press.uchicago.edu
www.press.uchicago.edu

© Policy Press 2016

British Library Cataloguing in Publication Data
A catalogue record for this book is available from the British Library.

Library of Congress Cataloging-in-Publication Data
A catalog record for this book has been requested.

ISBN 978-1-4473-3196-4 (hardcover)
ISBN 978-1-4473-3198-8 (ePub)
ISBN 978-1-4473-3199-5 (Mobi)
ISBN 978-1-4473-3197-1 (ePdf)

Cover design by Policy Press
Front cover: image kindly supplied by iStock

Contents

Acknowledgements

We wish to thank all the participants in this study, who came forward to share their individual stories. Also, we wish to thank Tell MAMA for their support throughout this study.

Irene Zempi and Imran Awan

About the authors

Irene Zempi is the Director of the Nottingham Centre for Study and Reduction of Bias, Prejudice and Hate Crime, and a Lecturer in Criminology at Nottingham Trent University.

Imran Awan is an Associate Professor in Criminology and Deputy Director of the Centre for Applied Criminology at Birmingham City University.

1
UNDERSTANDING ISLAMOPHOBIA

The term Islamophobia has come under increasing scrutiny after the rise in Islamophobic hate crimes post 9/11 and more recently following the Paris attacks in 2015. Both these incidents have led to a rise in Islamophobic hostility, and reported hate crimes committed against Muslim communities have increased (Littler and Feldman, 2015). As a result, Islamophobia has become an important and emerging concept, and it relates to wider issues around the racialisation and the 'othering' of Muslim communities. However, whilst there is no universal interpretation or definition of Islamophobia, the debate about what the term means is often stoked up by people's fears about Muslims. For example, increasingly the term 'Islamophobic hate crime' is used within the context of Muslims suffering a form of hate crime. Despite these debates in the United Kingdom (UK), it is acknowledged that hate crime is not always motivated by hate; rather, it can be motivated because of hostility or prejudice towards a person's disability, race or ethnicity, religion or belief, sexual orientation or transgender identity. This chapter focuses on the concepts and terminology surrounding Islamophobia and hate crime, and argues that contemporary Islamophobia is a reflection of a historical Islamophobic phenomenon which was constructed in colonial times, but which has increased significantly in recent times, creating a deeper resentment, hostility and fear of Islam and of Muslims than existed before.

Constructing the debate on Islamophobia

The Runnymede Trust described Islamophobia as unfounded hostility towards Muslims which results in fear and dislike of Muslims. The seminal Runnymede Trust report (1997) identified eight components of Islamophobia. They include where people view:

1. Islam as a faith that is unresponsive to change.
2. Where the values of Islam appear not to be compatible with other cultures and faiths.
3. Islam is viewed as being a religion that is barbaric and sexist.
4. Islam is also seen as being a religion that is both violent and aggressive.
5. Islam is viewed as a political ideology.
6. Islam and criticisms made about the faith are unwarranted.
7. Discriminatory practices are used to justify exclusion of Muslim communities.
8. Islamophobia is seen as normal.

They also argue that Islamophobic views are shaped by a 'closed set' of narrow views on Islam and Muslims, which has helped contribute to the 'othering' of Muslim communities through discriminative practices (Awan, 2012). The Forum against Islamophobia and Racism (2013) argue that Islamophobia constitutes fear and hostility against Muslim communities. However, like the above interpretations, they confine Islamophobia to physical attacks such as abuse and targeted violence against Muslim communities, mosques, cemeteries and discrimination in places of education (Allen, 2010). Islam therefore is seen as 'dangerous' because of the 'expansion' of Muslim communities. Whilst these definitions remain limited in scope with regards to the online dimension of Islamophobia, they do however provide a starting point for further analysis in this area.

According to Taras (2012), Islamophobia has become a term that is misunderstood and indeed lacking in clarity. Taras (2012: 4) states that Islamophobia entails 'the spread of hostile public attitudes towards

Muslims, in this case across Europe. The spread of Islamophobia is based on a conviction that Europe is in peril because of Islamisation'. For Taras (2012), his sense of securitisation and fear is about how visual representations of Islam have become synonymous with people who fear the pervading sense of history. For example, the construction of mosques, headscarves and minarets helps contribute towards the 'othering' of such communities. Along similar lines, Cole and Maisuria (2007: 103) argue that 'It is the visible symbols of Islam that are being attacked'. Taras (2012: 4) notes that 'Islamophobia thus entails a cultural racism that sets Muslims apart. As a result, the Islamic migrant is constructed as someone burdened by alien attributes and as a carrier of antagonistic, threatening values'. For Cole and Maisuria (2007), Islamophobia is a product of racism, and therefore racist abuse can also be viewed in the lens of Muslims being a 'risky' group. They state that 'Islamophobia, like other forms of racism, can be cultural or it can be biological, or it can be a mixture of both' (Cole and Maisuria, 2007: 106). Furthermore, they add that 'The racist term, "Paki" coexists with the racist term of abuse, "Bin Laden", and Islamic headscarves – hijabs – are now a symbol for a "cause for concern"' (Cole and Maisuria, 2007: 103).

It should be noted here that Islamophobia did not come into existence post 9/11. Muslims as a group have suffered from marginalisation and faced high risk of being victims of racially motivated crimes prior to this, including after the 'Cold War' (Chakraborti and Garland, 2009: 44). However, the recent events tend to show a sharp increase in reprisal attacks against Muslims. For example, McGhee (2005) found an increase in racist attacks reported to the police because of the way Muslims looked. Similarly, Muslims have faced a backlash whether it was in Europe (Modood, 2003) or the United States (US) (Perry, 2003), with a widespread range of Islamophobic attacks being reported. Allen and Nielsen (2002) found that Muslims who are visibly identifiable were more likely to be targeted by incidents of hate crime. Cole and Maisuria (2007: 104) argue that Muslims who are visibly identifiable are more likely to be discriminated against because of their appearance. They state that 'People who appear to be of Islamic faith (wearing a veil, sporting a beard, or even carrying a backpack (see Austin, 2006: 21)) are immediately identified as potential terrorists' (Cole and Maisuria, 2007: 104). The Woolwich attack also triggered a backlash against Muslims mainly because of the generalisation that all Muslims are potential terrorists.

Whilst Islamophobia has been viewed as a new term, it has long roots back from the time of the Christian Crusades to the Prophet Muhammad (Allen, 2010). Taras (2012: 119) notes how 'Islamophobia is a backlash to the expanded presence of Muslim communities in Europe'. Indeed, a recent BBC Radio 1 Newsbeat poll found that one in four young people in Britain distrust Muslims. Additionally, 16 per cent said they did not trust Hindus or Sikhs, 15 per cent said they did not trust Jewish people, 13 per cent said they did not trust Buddhists and 12 per cent said they did not trust Christians. Indeed, 44 per cent said that Muslims did not share the same values, whilst 28 per cent said the UK would be a better place with fewer Muslims there (Kotecha, 2013).

Prejudice towards Muslim communities post events such as 9/11, 7/7 and more recently the Woolwich attack has intensified. Sheridan's (2006) study of the impact of Islamophobia post and pre 9/11 found that Muslim communities had been targets for a range of Islamophobic abuse. This study investigated levels of self-reported racial and religious discrimination in a sample of 222 British Muslims, post September 2001. Sheridan (2006) found that levels of implicit or indirect discrimination rose by 82.6 per cent and experiences of overt discrimination by 76.3 per cent. Sheridan (2006: 317) states that 'Thus, the current work demonstrates that major world events may affect not only stereotypes of minority groups but also prejudice toward minorities. Results suggest that religious affiliation may be a more meaningful predictor of prejudice than race or ethnicity'. Below is a direct quote from the study by Sheridan (2006: 332) with a Muslim male student who had suffered Islamophobic hostility:

'I was traveling on the bus and about to open up my bag when a voice from behind me said "Go on then, take out that bomb!"

He repeatedly told me to "F***OFF back to my country". He said repeatedly that I don't belong here. He accused me and "my people" to be behind the (September 11th) attacks. He tried to racially incite the other passengers against me. He kept swearing at me and said things like, "why do you keep a beard?? Tell everyone!!!" He got up a few times and came close to me as if he was going to become physical but at the end sat back down. One of the worst things was that NOBODY was saying anything to him. It was as if they cared more about their own safety. Some shook their heads disapprovingly but that didn't help me at all but in fact their silence helped him instead!'

Githens-Mazer and Lambert (2010: 38) cite the case of a man shouting 'f****** terrorist c***' at a Muslim woman who was waiting at a bus stop from his van window. They state that 'Immediately prior to hearing this abuse the victim had been struck on the chin by phlegm that her unknown assailant spat at her'. Githens-Mazer and Lambert (2010: 38) argue that 'Another important aspect of routine, everyday anti-Muslim hate crime is anonymous telephone, email and postal death threats and threats of harm. Indeed, on occasion they require to be classified as serious hate crimes. Since 9/11, hundreds of death threats, threats of serious physical harm, along with more general violent threats and abuse. Death threats may be closely related to threats of serious harm made by the same individual or on behalf of the same group or organisation. Finally, death threats may be made by an individual or group known to the victim or they may be made anonymously by a variety of means, by an unknown individual sometimes on behalf of a group or organisation that may also be known or unknown'.

This isolation and marginalisation of Muslim communities appear to be rooted in the narrative that Islam is a barbaric faith and that Islam and the West are, in actual fact, involved in a clash of civilisations (Huntington, 1996). This belief often creates the space whereby Muslims are targeted and also vilified for their faith, both offline and online. This demonisation is captured in studies with Muslim communities conducted by Awan (2012) and Zempi (2014), which looked at online Islamophobia and the demonisation of veiled Muslim women, respectively. Their studies found that Muslims were being targeted both online and offline, which had culminated in Muslims feeling isolated and alienated.

Online Islamophobia

Islamophobic hate crime falls under the category of religious hate crime, which is where it is perceived, by the victim or any other person, to be motivated by a hostility or prejudice based upon a person's religion or perceived religion (Keats, 2014). Online Islamophobia can be defined as Islamophobic prejudice that targets a victim in order to provoke, cause hostility and promote intolerance by means of harassment, stalking, abuse, incitement, threatening behaviour, bullying and intimidation of the person or persons, via all platforms of social media. In particular, post Woolwich and the death of drummer Lee Rigby in the UK, evidence shows that there has been an increase in online Islamophobia (Awan, 2014; 2016).

Online hate can come in many different forms and shapes, from racial harassment, religiously motivated abuse, including Islamophobic abuse, anti-Semitic abuse and directed abuse more generally which targets someone because of their disability, gender, culture, race and beliefs (Gerstenfeld, 2013). Cyberspace therefore becomes a virtual minefield where offenders or 'trolls or trolling' specifically target people through online premeditated abuse and specific targeting of a victim, which a perpetrator has identified (Perry and Olsson, 2009). The internet troll specifically aims to target and harass an individual(s) because of their perceived difference. In effect, the internet troll aims to use cyberspace as a means to create a hostile space where online hate can permeate (Perry, 2001). In the virtual world, the use of social media can have profound consequences when misused and allows perpetrators a safe space to create a hostile virtual environment by using threatening messages. For example, the freelance journalist Caroline Criado-Perez, was subjected to abusive threats, which included rape, via Twitter. Some of the comments posted online included 'Everyone jump on the rape train, @CCriadoPerez is the conductor' and 'Hey sweetheart, give me a call when you're ready to be put in your place' (cited online in *The Huffington Post*, 2013).

In the policing context, tackling online hate speech requires strong partnership work with the Crown Prosecution Service (CPS). Communications sent via social media sites, like Twitter, can also be a criminal offence. The CPS guidelines published in 2013 state that there must be either a credible threat of violence or communications which specifically target an individual or group of people, communications which amount to a breach of a court order and communications which may be considered grossly offensive, indecent, obscene or false (CPS, 2013). In many of these cases, people can be charged for comments made via social networking sites under 'racially motivated' or 'religiously motivated' crimes through the Crime and Disorder Act 1998, the Malicious Communications Act 1988, the Communications Act 2003 and the Public Order Act 1986 (Coliandris, 2012).

Following the Woolwich attack, a number of arrests were made where people had posted comments on Twitter and Facebook, which were deemed to incite racial hatred or violence. In one case, a person was convicted under the Malicious Communications Act 1988 after an offensive message was posted on Facebook (Urquhart, 2013). At the moment, cyberspace does resemble a virtual minefield of hate and therefore policing it requires a shift in thinking from authorities which gets them thinking and acting not in an abstract 'black and white' way, but in a more innovative and nuanced way that helps the police prosecute people for cyber hate, as well as educating people of the dangers of online abuse (Chan, 2007).

Offline Islamophobia

In terms of offline Islamophobia, Muslims have also been victims of physical abuse, assaults, verbal abuse, mosques being targeted and Muslim women being spat at and having their veils being pulled off (Awan, 2014; Zempi, 2014). This has emerged after incidents such as Woolwich and Paris, and more recently this level of impact upon Muslims has been immense. Mythen et al's (2009) study investigated the effects of Islamophobic hate crime and security processes on young British Pakistanis in the north-west of England. Their study involved a series of four focus group sessions in different venues with 32 British Muslims, and found that young British Muslims related their experiences of victimisation. Mythen et al (2009: 742) state that:

> …victimisation is understood as both the act by which someone is rendered a victim, the experience of being a victim alongside the sociocultural process by which this takes place. This broad understanding allows for victimisation to be ideological (that is pertaining to ideas and values that victimise individuals or groups) and to have material consequences for those that are victimised (for example through verbal abuse or physical assault).

Githens-Mazer and Lambert's (2010) study found that a number of Muslim Londoners had also been the victims of hate crimes since 9/11. They also found that a number of incidents were not reported to the police. They state that 'While some of the more serious attacks of the kind we have illustrated have been reported to police, the overwhelming majority of Muslim victims of hate crimes appear not to have reported the incidents to police. Sometimes, interviewees suggest, that failure to report a crime to police is because of a lack of confidence in the police and other times because of a failure to appreciate that an incident merits police attention' (Githens-Mazer and Lambert, 2010: 38).

In light of these points, it can be argued that since the emergence of events such as 9/11, 7/7, Woolwich and Paris, there has been an increase in hate crimes committed against Muslim communities. Whilst many of these incidents have led to offline violence, there is also a sense that such incidents are now common place online. Indeed, the debate about what constitutes a hate crime and the rationale for using terminology such as Islamophobia has often shed more heat than light. This chapter has explored those key concepts and argues that whilst terms are important for conceptualising certain types of crimes, they also do not take into account the 'real' life stories and cases of people who are often victims of such incidents. The manifestation of Islamophobia online has resulted in debates about how we conceptualise the term and also the impact of such incidents upon the victims. These attacks online mean that the police, social media companies and government must do more to tackle online Islamophobic hate crime. Social media and the internet provide safe online spaces which have created a vacuum for perpetrators to target vulnerable people by using anti-Semitic abuse, racist abuse, homophobic abuse, gender-based abuse, anti-disability abuse and Islamophobic abuse. As a result, online Islamophobic hate crime has also been increasing and there is an urgent need to examine the implications this has for individual victims, their families and wider Muslim communities.

Understanding hate crime

There is no universal definition of a hate crime, although we have a myriad of interpretations and examples of terms that have been used to define what might constitute a hate crime. In the UK, a hate crime is any criminal offence which is perceived, by the victim or any other person, to be motivated by a hostility or prejudice based on a person's race or perceived race, because of their disability, race or ethnicity, religion or belief, sexual orientation or transgender identity. Garland and Chakraborti (2012) make the case that potential victims of hate crime are targeted because of their status and perceived affiliation with specific groups. They state that 'Linked to this is the question of whether offenders target potential victims because of their membership of despised "outgroups", irrespective of who they are as individuals, or whether many offenders, at least to a degree, actually know their victims' (Garland and Chakraborti, 2012: 40). Craig (2002) states that this equates to any illegal act, which intentionally selects a victim because of those prejudices against the victim. This type of crime can also be committed against a person or property and the victim does not have to be a member of the group at which the hostility is targeted. Indeed, the notion that an offender must be motivated by hate for there to be a hate crime is problematic.

Chakraborti and Garland (2009: 4) make the case that 'in reality crimes do not need to be motivated by hatred at all'. Similarly, Hall (2013: 9) states that 'Hate crime isn't really about hate, but about criminal behaviour motivated by prejudice, of which hate is just one small and extreme part', which does raise important questions about rethinking what hate crime actually means. Referring to the impact of hate crime Iganski (2001: 628) suggests that:

> It scars the victim far more deeply. It is much more difficult I think as a victim to say I was put in the hospital because I'm gay or because I'm Hispanic, or because I'm a woman, than it is to say, you know I was walking down the street and I had my bag around my arm and some guy snatched from me, some guy knocked me over the head and took what I had, because they want property. You're not being singled out. You are beaten or hurt because of who you are.

Perry (2001: 10) argues that hate crime is about offenders pursuing a level of control and power, and states that a hate crime must involve:

> [...]acts of violence and intimidation, usually directed towards already stigmatized and marginalized groups. As such it is a mechanism of power and oppression, intended to reaffirm the precarious hierarchies that characterize a given social order. It attempts to re-create simultaneously the threatened (real or imagined) hegemony of the perpetrator's group and the appropriate subordinate identity of the victim's group. It is a means of marking both the Self and the Other in such a way as to re-establish their 'proper' relative positions, as given and reproduced by broader ideologies and patterns of social and political inequality.

Iganski (2001: 634) argues that:

> There has been a great deal of speculation about what the harms might be but relatively little empirical investigation. And, not all of the alleged harms provide a justification for the additional punishment of a class of crimes. For instance, it has been observed that hate crimes are more likely to involve 'excessive violence' (B. Levin, 1999, p. 15); cause injury; lead to hospitalization; and involve multiple offenders, serial attacks, and repeat victimization of the same targets than criminal assaults in general (B. Levin, 1999, p. 15; J. Levin & McDevitt, 1993). Although these harms would obviously merit more severe penalties in the specific cases to which they apply, none of them arguably provides a justification for the creation of a category of punishment above and beyond the circumstances of the particular crime.

Chakraborti and Garland (2009: 6) note how Perry's definition extends to all 'members and groups' who are victimised and marginalised, and as such, they argue that Perry's definition provides a more fluid and comprehensive interpretation of the meaning of hate crime. They state that 'Crucially, it recognises that hate crime is not a static problem but one that is historically and culturally contingent, the experience of which needs to be seen as a dynamic process, involving context, structure and agency'. With respect to the motivation element surrounding the term, Hall (2013: 3) makes the case that:

> In this sense then it is society's interest in the motivation that lies behind the commission of the crime that is new. That motivation is, of course, an offender's hatred of, or more accurately, prejudice against, a particular identifiable group or member of a particular identifiable group, usually already marginalized within society, whom the offender intentionally selects on the basis of that prejudice.

Similarly, Gerstenfeld (2013: 9) argues that hate crime has no borders and therefore we cannot simply measure it through domestic problems but that instead it requires an international approach that involves working with wider partners such as the United Nations, the European Union and the Organisation for Security and Cooperation in Europe (OSCE) to share ideas, experience and good practice that can help tackle the problem of hate crime.

Indeed, the convergence of hate crime and Islamophobia on the internet has provided a new platform by which a number of websites and groups have appeared online in order to perpetuate a level of cyber hate not seen previously. The UK policy and legal interpretation of hate crime has divided the term into different areas from hate motivation, hate incidents and hate crimes. The operational definition in England and Wales states that hate motivation is where: 'Hate crimes and incidents are taken to mean any crime or incident where the perpetrator's hostility or prejudice against an identifiable group of people is a factor in determining who is victimised' (College of Policing, 2014: 3). The definition included here is broader in the sense that the victim does not have to be a member of a group. A hate incident on the other hand is described as 'Any non-crime incident which is perceived by the victim or any other person, to be motivated by a hostility or prejudice based on a person's race or perceived race, religion or perceived religion, sexual orientation or perceived sexual orientation, disability or perceived disability, or transgender or perceived to be transgender' (College of Policing, 2014: 3). In this context, the victims could be classified as any racial group or ethnic background which includes countries within the UK and 'Gypsy and Traveller groups' and any other religious group including those who have no faith. Furthermore, Garland and Chakraborti (2012: 41) state that 'Linked to this is the suggestion that hate crimes are more hurtful than "everyday" crimes lacking the bias motive. Because they target cultural, ethnic, religious or sexual identity, for instance, these acts damage feelings of self-worth and security...'.

Cyber hate therefore, is a nexus of those communications and concepts where a perpetrator utilises electronic technology and the convergence of space, movement and behaviour in a 'safe' virtual environment to 'control' and target 'opponents' considered to be a threat (Awan and Blakemore, 2012). This type of control allows the perpetrator to act in a dominant way against groups they deem to be subordinate, often as is the case with Muslims, attacking their faith and ethnicity (Perry, 2001). It also allows offenders to use the online world and other social networking platforms to target individuals they deem to be 'different' from them in an ideological, political and religious sense (Cole and Cole, 2009).

RESEARCH METHODS

This chapter presents the methodology of this study and the rationale for using in-depth interviews when researching Islamophobia. It highlights the core epistemological and methodological assumptions that characterise qualitative research. Also, it discusses the practicalities of the present methodology, including developing the interview guide, establishing rapport and trust with participants, and analysing the research data using the principles of grounded theory. This is followed by a discussion of reflexivity, which outlines how the researchers' positionality and subjectivity might have influenced the research process.

Overview of research design

The research took the form of a qualitative study based on individual, in-depth interviews with Muslim men and women between May and August 2015. Specifically, we interviewed 20 individuals who had been victims of both online and offline Islamophobia in the UK. Participation to the study was voluntary. The interviews, undertaken by the authors, typically ranged from one to two hours, with an average interview length of one hour. All interviews were digitally recorded, transcribed verbatim and then analysed using grounded theory. The research aims and objectives of the study were: (a) to examine the nature and extent of online and offline Islamophobia directed towards Muslims in the UK; (b) to understand the factors that determine the prevalence and severity of online and offline Islamophobia; (c) to explore the impact of this hostility upon victims, their families and wider Muslim communities; (d) to offer recommendations in terms of preventing and responding to both online and offline Islamophobia.

The study employed purposive sampling, which is a non-random method of participant recruitment. Prospective participants were Muslims who had reported their online and offline experiences of Islamophobia to Tell MAMA. Launched in 2012, the Tell MAMA programme is a non-profit organisation that is coordinated and implemented by an interfaith organisation, Faith Matters. Tell MAMA offers services to individuals who have suffered Islamophobic attacks. It operates as an alternative reporting system on the basis that if victims want the attack logged and passed on to the police (but they do not wish to contact the police themselves), Tell MAMA will do this on their behalf. Individuals can report to Tell MAMA in various ways including via a Freephone number, SMS, Facebook, Twitter, e-mail and online. Tell MAMA contributes to supplementing official statistics through a variety of reporting mechanisms, including the use of social networking sites. The process of identifying prospective participants included Tell MAMA contacting people who had reported both online and offline incidents of Islamophobia to them in 2015. Once individuals confirmed their interest to Tell MAMA in terms of participating in the present study, their details were passed on to us, and we subsequently engaged directly with them for conducting the interviews. An advantage of employing Tell MAMA for participant recruitment was that individuals were introduced to the study by a familiar, trusted organisation. This alleviated any concerns that participants might have had about taking part in the study, thus potentially increasing participation in the study.

Using purposive sampling was appropriate for accessing our target population. As Bryman (2008) points out, this method of recruiting participants is particularly useful for accessing 'hard-to-reach' groups that may be difficult to identify with other recruitment methods. Generally speaking, purposive sampling can be understood as deliberate and flexible. It is deliberate because of selecting 'on purpose' people who are 'information-rich' on the study topic (Hennink et al, 2011: 85). To illustrate this, all participants who had contacted Tell MAMA had experiences of both online and offline Islamophobia. Therefore, they could provide detailed accounts of the nature and extent of both online and offline Islamophobia. Purposive sampling is also flexible in terms of seeking a diverse range of participants who can provide a variety of experiences on the study topic rather than following a rigid recruitment procedure from the outset (Hennink et al, 2011). Indeed, this diversity is depicted in the pool of participants recruited.

For example, out of the 20 participants, there were 11 female and nine male individuals. With respect to age, the majority of participants were aged between 20-30 years (seven participants aged 20 and over, and eight participants aged 30 and over), with four participants aged 40 and over, and one participant aged 50. The youngest participant was aged 20 and the oldest was 50. With respect to ethnicity, we had a broad and diverse group, which was comprised of people from different racial and ethnic backgrounds. Participants included those from Asian heritage (11), White British convert (five), Somalian (three) and Libyan (one). A common characteristic amongst all the participants was the fact that they were 'visibly' Muslim. This means that they could be identified as practising Muslims particularly through their appearance. For example, the female participants were 'visibly' Muslim through wearing the jilbab, hijab and/or niqab. The male participants were 'visibly' Muslim because they had a beard, wore the traditional Islamic clothing and/or a cap. Moreover, participants could be identified as practising Muslims because of their name, and/or comments that they had made online.

Due to the in-depth nature of qualitative research, few study participants were needed, as the purpose was to achieve depth of information (rather than breadth), by gaining a detailed understanding of underlying beliefs, views and opinions. Indeed, qualitative research is not intended to be representative of the general population (Silverman, 2013). This means that it is not possible to quantify the data and/or extrapolate the present findings to a broader population. As such, our sample does not cover the full spectrum of experiences, views and opinions that might be held by Muslims who have experienced online and/or offline Islamophobia. Similarly, the sample is not representative of the thousands of victims who have contacted Tell MAMA to report their experiences of Islamophobia. Moreover, the study did not speak to perpetrators. Although this aspect was deliberately excluded from the parameters of this study, it is evident that we do not actually know the motivations that drove the perpetrators to commit the acts that they did. Rather, we have to rely on victims' testimony in order to draw conclusions about offenders' motivations. These limitations do not undermine the significance of the study, but it is clear that future research should explore them in more depth.

With respect to ethics, the study underwent a formal assessment by our Institutional Review Boards and Ethics Committees respectively, and was granted approval. Participants were provided with relevant information about the study and made a voluntary decision to take part in the study. Participants had the right to determine their participation in the study, including the right to refuse participation without any negative consequences. All data records were kept confidential at all times by keeping the acquired information secure and by replacing participants' names with pseudonyms to preserve their anonymity.

Qualitative interviewing

Qualitative research is used for providing in-depth understanding of people's underlying views, beliefs and motivations. Qualitative research has been defined by Denzin and Lincoln (2000: 3) as:

> […]a situated activity that locates the observer in the world. It consists of a set of interpretive, material practices that make the world visible. These practices transform the world. They turn the world into a series of representations, including field notes, interviews, conversations, photographs, and recordings, and memos to the self.

2. RESEARCH METHODS

Qualitative research produces in-depth, subjective accounts from which it is possible to ascertain the beliefs, attitudes and experiences of the study participants (Silverman, 2013). Qualitative research looks beyond the surface and explores people's views, beliefs and motivations by asking them to reflect and share stories about their experiences. From this perspective, qualitative methods are particularly suitable for examining sensitive topics such as victimisation, on the basis that the process of rapport building provides a comfortable atmosphere for participant disclosure (Hennink et al, 2011). A qualitative approach was employed in the present study as it is particularly effective for capturing the experiences, views and opinions of people who have experienced Islamophobia. Specifically, using a qualitative approach allowed us to understand the views, behaviours and feelings from the perspective of study participants themselves. Additionally, using a qualitative approach helped us to give 'voice' to a marginalised group in society, which is also 'invisible' in research terms. Also, using a qualitative approach allowed us to examine in detail a new and complex issue, specifically online and offline Islamophobia, and the relationship between these two facets of Islamophobia. Within this framework, the use of in-depth interviews provided the study with detailed and diverse insights of participants' online and offline experiences of Islamophobia, as well as information about the nature, causes and impacts of this form of hate crime.

As mentioned above, the present study involved in-depth interviews with Muslim men and women who had experienced both online and offline Islamophobia. An in-depth interview is a one-to-one method of data collection that involves an interviewer and an interviewee discussing a topic in depth (Hennink et al, 2011). In-depth interviews can be described as a conversation with a purpose, although it should not be understood as a two-way dialogue, as only the interviewee shares their story and the interviewer's role is to elicit the story. As such, in-depth interviews allow for 'rich' or 'thick' data to be collected with detailed descriptions (Curtis and Curtis, 2011). It is especially valuable for providing the information in sufficient depth and attuning it to the varying levels of comprehension present in the target population.

The interviews were semi-structured, and tailored to meet the specific requirements of each particular interviewee. Semi-structured interview formats predefine to some extent the research agenda but enable respondents some freedom to present a range of views and offer new insights (Payne, 2004). In this regard, interview questions are not static; rather, they change, are adapted and refined during fieldwork. As such, semi-structured interviewing is a flexible method of data collection in terms of changing the order of interview questions, following up interesting points raised by interviewees, including material that the participants brought up that the interviewer might not have anticipated, and clearing up inconsistencies in answers (Maxfield and Babbie, 2009). This approach provides an opportunity for participants' 'voices' to be heard and for them to raise issues of salience, which are not necessarily part of the research agenda (Payne, 2004).

Furthermore, it is important to point out that qualitative methods include a range of approaches that are based on different epistemologies. Epistemology explores issues such as 'what the relationship is between the inquirer and the known' (Denzin and Lincoln, 2008: 31) and 'what might represent knowledge or evidence of the social reality that is investigated (Mason, 2002: 16). These different philosophical positions/theories of knowledge have implications for how data are collected, how data are regarded during analysis, what claims are made for the findings and even how the different methods should be evaluated (Payne, 2004). The framework which was used to guide the research design and data collection in the present study was grounded theory (Glaser and Strauss, 1967), where themes were allowed to emerge from the data, thereby enabling theories about the nature and extent of online and offline Islamophobia to be generated, tested and refined during the analytical process.

Grounded theory is not a theory itself; rather, it is a process for developing empirical theory from qualitative research that consists of a set of tasks and underlying principles (Hennink et al, 2011). Within a grounded theory framework, participants' responses are construed as evidence of what they think and feel and how they interpret their world (Glaser, 1992). Grounded theory, which is based on an inductive approach, involves developing a 'story' that emerges from the data. In this case, a verbatim transcript is essential for grounded theory analysis, as it captures information in participants' own words, phrases and expressions as well as providing 'rich' detail. From a methodological perspective, the use of quotations can be seen as a means of validating the issues reported to show that they were indeed evident in the data in the way the researcher(s) described; thus, the use of quotations can be an effective tool to demonstrate validity (Hennink et al, 2011).

Correspondingly, in this study we used participants' direct quotations in order to illustrate the themes emerging from the analysis, provide evidence for our interpretations and offer readers greater depth of understanding. This approach empowers participants by inclusion of their spoken words. Using quotations from the study participants represents a philosophical tradition to empower the study population by giving 'voice' to their issues. Finlay (2002: 541) argues that 'the researcher's position can become unduly privileged, blocking out the participant's voice'. Throughout this study, our aim was to focus on capturing research issues from the perspective of the participants themselves and make their 'voices' evident in the findings. In this regard, using quotations from the participants enabled us to understand their views in their own words, interpret the meanings and form conclusions that were well rooted in the data.

Reflexivity

The positivism paradigm, which is typically seen as the scientific approach to research, emphasises the objective measurement of social issues. From this perspective, it is assumed that reality consists of facts, and that researchers can observe and measure reality in an objective way with no influence of the researcher on the process of data collection (Hennink et al, 2011). As such, positivism assumes research to be value free on the basis that there is a 'separation of facts from values' (Charmaz, 2006: 5). However, positivism is often criticised for its assumptions about objective measurement, which separates the researcher from the researched, and for failing to recognise the interactive and co-constructive nature of data collection with research participants (Hennink et al, 2011).

Payne (2004) observes that the terms and concepts used to demonstrate rigour in quantitative research – including reliability, validity, representativeness, generalisability and objectivity – are problematic for qualitative research. Since most qualitative research methods of analysis are concerned with the interpretation of data, and the researcher's role in this is explicitly acknowledged, the dichotomy between subjectivity and objectivity is not supportable. Rather, qualitative researchers must demonstrate the methodological rigour of their work, and be clear and explicit in the claims made when research is written up or presented. In this regard, using reflexivity enables researchers to achieve this by acknowledging their role in the creation of the analytical account. According to Green and Thorogood (2004: 195), reflexivity encourages 'methodological openness' whereby researchers reflect on how the data were 'made', for example, researchers' decisions that may have influenced the data.

Reflexivity, which entails an awareness of self within the process of data collection and analysis, is regarded as an important element in demonstrating the rigour of qualitative analysis (Payne, 2004). In particular, reflexivity is a process that involves conscious self-reflection on the part of the researchers in order to make explicit their potential influence on the research process (Hennink et al, 2011). According to Pillow (2003), reflexivity is necessary in order to legitimise and validate the research process. In this regard, the researcher 'understands that he is part of the social world(s) that he or she investigates' (Berg, 2007: 178). This indicates that researchers need to use reflexivity throughout the research process in order to recognise the potential influence of the researcher(s) on the research design, participant selection, as well as data collection and interpretation (Hennink et al, 2011). Correspondingly, throughout the research cycle, we asked for feedback from our research participants, and received critical remarks on the research design, which we implemented; thus enhancing the quality of the study. For example, we found that interview questions posed in a more academic language were not immediately understandable by some participants and thus we decided to pose questions in colloquial language. Amending the language of the questions posed was important in order to get an insight into participants' perceptions, emotions, feelings and beliefs, and thus truly understand their experiences.

According to Hammersley and Atkinson (1983), an interview is a 'social event' where responses are not simply given to the questions but also to the researcher who poses those questions coupled with participants' perceptions of the researcher. In this regard, qualitative interviewing is a two-way learning process where both the researcher and the researched participate in this knowledge-building activity, while at the same time, responding to specific perceived subjectivities (Shah, 2004). We agree with Hesse-Biber and Leavy (2006: 128) who describe in-depth interviewing as a 'meaning-making partnership between interviewees and their respondents' thereby indicating that in-depth interviews are 'a special kind of knowledge-producing conversation'. In this case, the researcher(s) and the researched co-construct reality through co-creating knowledge and meaning in the interview setting. Relatedly, it could be argued that this study was conducted from an outsider's perspective. Imran has been investigating Islamophobia for the last decade. Although he is a Muslim, Imran has never experienced Islamophobic abuse in public, possibly because his Muslim identity is not 'visible'. Therefore, although he could be perceived as an 'insider' based on his religion, he could also be seen as an 'outsider' on the basis of his non-visible Muslim identity. For Irene, being an Orthodox Christian female researcher meant that she was perceived as an 'outsider' by her participants due to her religion.

In insider research, the researcher conducts research with a group of which he or she is a member, based on characteristics such as religion, race/ethnicity, gender and sexual identity (Kanuha, 2000). Insider research is considered to be from an emic perspective, as it involves the description of a phenomenon that is understood by the researcher who has also experienced it (Spiers, 2000). A common argument in the research literature is that insiders are more likely to be able to understand and accurately represent participants' experiences (Labaree,

2002). This can be particularly useful in research with groups that have been underrepresented and socially or culturally marginalised. Typically, outsider researchers are accused of lacking understanding (Savvides et al, 2014). From this perspective, outsiders cannot understand or represent accurately the experiences of their participants. This is a particularly salient topic when research is conducted with oppressed, marginalised and 'other' communities (Hayfield and Huxley, 2015). In order to gain an insider's perspective we used different techniques such as using a semi-structured interview guide to prompt the data collection; employing careful listening skills, establishing rapport and trust with participants; creating a safe, comfortable environment for participants; asking questions in an open, unthreatening way and in a friendly colloquial manner; showing empathy towards participants; and motivating them to tell their stories in detail by using probes.

All of the participants reported that they actually enjoyed participating in the study as it provided a rare opportunity for them to talk about their lived experiences of online and offline Islamophobia in a safe environment. Many referred to the cathartic value of taking part in this research project. However, there were times during the interview when participants often had to revisit painful memories or events in their lives, which could cause emotional distress. We were aware of the fact that the process of qualitative interviewing on sensitive issues often evokes emotional responses from participants and we were prepared to terminate the interview in cases where emotional distress was caused to participants. In cases where the interview caused some emotional stress to participants, we dealt with this empathy. At the same time though, we were aware of our limited abilities in assisting participants (for example, we are researchers rather than trained counsellors) and thus we provided participants with information about receiving professional support through their GP, victim support and the Samaritans.

3
TRIGGERS OF ISLAMOPHOBIC VIOLENCE

This chapter examines the factors that determine the prevalence and severity of Islamophobic violence such as 'trigger' events of local, national and international significance. Correspondingly, the study participants reported that the prevalence of both online and offline Islamophobic hate crimes increased following recent high-profile terrorist attacks around the world such as Sydney, Paris, Copenhagen and Tunisia. Additionally, national scandals such as the grooming of young girls in Rotherham by groups of Pakistani men and the alleged 'Trojan Horse' scandal in Birmingham, framed as a 'jihadist plot' to take over schools, were also highlighted as 'trigger' events. The 'visibility' and intersectionality of victims' identities also emerged as contributing factors to manifestations of Islamophobia, both online and offline.

Terrorist acts – national and international

Recent research shows that the prevalence and severity of Islamophobic hate crimes are influenced in the short term by singular, or clusters of, events. From this perspective, Islamophobic hate crimes increase following 'trigger' events as they operate to galvanise tensions and sentiments against the suspected perpetrators and groups associated with them. Specifically, terrorist acts appear to function as antecedent 'trigger' events that 'validate' prejudicial sentiments and tensions, thereby promoting the spread of hostile beliefs and the mobilisation of action as a result of the desire for retribution in the targeted group (Williams and Burnap, 2015). This manifests in the escalation of hostility towards groups that share similar characteristics to the perpetrators.

Indeed, evidence demonstrates that Islamophobic hate crimes have increased significantly following 'trigger' terrorist attacks carried out by individuals who choose to identify themselves as being Muslim or acting in the name of Islam. King and Sutton (2014) found an association between the 9/11 terrorist attacks and a rise in hate crime incidents with a specific anti-Islamic motive in the US. In the UK, Hanes and Machin (2014) found significant increases in Islamophobic hate crimes reported to the police in London following 9/11 and 7/7. Both studies highlight a sharp de-escalation following the spike in Islamophobic hate crimes, which occurred as a result of the 'trigger' terrorist events. Spikes in Islamophobic hate crimes and incidents following 'trigger' terrorist events are not confined to the offline world; rather, the offline world pattern is replicated in the online world (Awan, 2014). For example, Williams and Burnap (2015) found that racial and religious cyber hate spiked in the immediate aftermath of the murder of Lee Rigby in the terrorist attack in Woolwich, London in 2013.[1] Littler and Feldman (2015) found that there was a substantial spike in reports of Islamophobic hate crime following the Woolwich attack, which ranged from general abuse towards 'visible' Muslims on the street, graffiti at mosques, firebombs at mosques to threats in a cyber context.

Britain's biggest force, the Metropolitan police, recorded 500 Islamophobic hate crimes following the Woolwich attack, whilst a similar picture emerged across the country with increased numbers of Islamophobic hate crimes reported by police in greater Manchester, Kent, Leicestershire, Thames Valley, Cheshire, Merseyside, West Yorkshire, Humberside, Nottinghamshire, Lancashire, Staffordshire,

---

[1] The British-born Muslim converts Michael Adebolajo and Michael Adebowale murdered Fusilier Lee Rigby at the Royal Artillery Barracks in Woolwich, south-east London on 22 May 2013. This was the first al-Qaida-inspired attack to claim a life on British soil since the 7/7 London terrorist attacks.

Cambridgeshire, Suffolk, Essex and Gloucestershire (Lazenby, 2013). Similarly, the Woolwich attack was cited by our participants as a terrorist antecedent 'trigger' event, which induced a significant increase in their online and offline experiences of Islamophobic violence, as the following comments illustrate.

'I know sisters who have been punched, being shouted at on the street, being pulled and pushed around by people, had their houses being burned down. These are the results of trigger events like when Lee Rigby was murdered.' (Sarah)

'I have figured out over the years that this happens when there is a terrorist attack in the news committed by Muslims so Islamophobia happens even more. A clear example is the Lee Rigby murder.' (Ahmed)

'There is an implicit assumption that all Muslims are responsible and thus we need to justify the murder of Lee Rigby by Adebolajo and Adebowale. We should not be held responsible for the actions of people who commit crimes in the name of Islam.' (Adam)

Moreover, participants reported that the prevalence and severity of both online and offline Islamophobic hate crimes increased following high-profile terrorist attacks around the world such as Sydney[2] in December 2014, the *Charlie Hebdo* attack in Paris[3] in January 2015,

---

[2] On 15-16 December 2014, Man Haron Monis, an Iranian-born Australian citizen, took hostages in a siege at the Lindt Chocolate Café at Martin Place, Sydney. The siege resulted in the death of Monis and two hostages.

[3] For three days (from 7-9 January 2015), a series of terrorist attacks occurred in Paris. On 7 January 2015, brothers Saïd and Chérif Kouachi forced their way into the offices of the French satirical weekly newspaper *Charlie Hebdo* in Paris and killed 11 people and injured 11 others in the building. After leaving, they killed a French National Police officer outside the building. On 9 January, police tracked the assailants to an industrial estate in Paris, where they took a hostage. Another gunman also shot a police officer on 8 January and took hostages the next day, at a kosher supermarket in Paris. The gunman was killed and four hostages were found dead.

attacks in Copenhagen[4] in February 2015 and Tunisia[5] in June 2015. Reflecting a spike in both online and offline Islamophobic hate crimes, participants reported that:

> 'Islamophobia does increase as soon as an incident occurs like the Paris attacks.' (Aisha)

> 'I have received Islamophobic abuse in social media and on the street on various occasions. After the Sydney incident, I received Islamophobic remarks on four separate occasions in the space of two weeks.' (Hamza)

> 'I was very nervous about what might happen following the Paris attacks. The anticipation is perhaps worse than the reality. After the Paris attacks, there were a lot of nasty comments especially on social media. I had to block some people on Facebook because of the comments they've made "Oh you are a paedophile" and all this nonsense.' (Asma)

Case study 1 highlights Jasmine's experiences of Islamophobia at a school where she was working as a mentor and teaching assistant.

Case study 1: Jasmine, 20 years old, white British convert

On my previous school placement (where I was a mentor/teaching assistant), children have engaged in discussion and told me that 'all Muslims are terrorists'. This was in front of teachers and went unchallenged. I discussed the views with the children and they became more abusive, saying we get our views from our 'terror religion'. I

---

[4] On 15 February 2015, a gunman opened fire on a synagogue, hours after one man was killed and three police officers wounded during an attack on a free speech event in the city.

[5] On 26 June 2015, a gunman attacked the beach resort of Sousse in Tunisia. ISIS claimed responsibility for the attack in which 38 people – plus the gunman – were killed. At least 15 of the victims were British.

asked them how they knew this and they said from the newspapers. I said perhaps this was biased, like it is about young people, but they said that I was wrong. Eventually, I was asked to leave the class and made to feel like I was causing the problem. On the same placement, the children were regularly using racial language unchallenged by the teachers. On my first, day my hijab was sharply pulled by a child, this was witnessed by a teacher and went unchallenged by them. On the placement I was made to pray in a storage cupboard where people kept their bikes, bags and which stored a kiln. One of the classrooms had a picture of Alan Henning – tied up with an ISIS person and a knife – on the wall. I challenged this and was told it was part of a child's artwork. I asked them how they would counteract the negative perceptions this was causing. I was told that it wasn't causing a problem to anyone else and to leave it. This could be seen clearly by the children, some of whom were 11 years old. I felt very uncomfortable working next to it. I was compared to the ISIS fighters by some children, and then I did not return to the school again.

Similar to Jasmine, other participants also referred to a spike in their experiences of online and offline Islamophobic hate crimes following the rise of the Islamic State of Iraq and Syria (ISIS). As the following quotations demonstrate, participants reported being 'bombarded with online and offline Islamophobic threats' with the prominence of ISIS, especially following the release of brutal videos showing beheadings carried out by ISIS or when there was a terror threat made against the UK from ISIS members.

'I keep my Facebook account private but I get a lot of abuse on Twitter especially if something has happened like when ISIS killed Alan Henning. I recently posted a comment on Channel 4 News webpage saying that the ISIS actions are bad and then I got loads and loads of abusive comments like "you are part of a terrorist religion".' (Sophie)

'I was on my way to the shops and people shouted at me "why don't we chop your head off?" In another case, people on the street shouted "your head will be much better on the floor".' (Sarah)

'The cancer of ISIS and the atrocities that Boko Haram commit in Nigeria, when these incidents happen anti-Muslim hate crime does rise too. On my birthday, a group of white men shouted at me and my sister "you Muslim scums, supporters of ISIS, tell us how much you hate Britain".' (Aisha)

'Obviously incidents like the Paris shootings and ISIS killings have a massive effect. It's like adding fuel to the fire.' (Ibrahim)

This indicates that in a globally connected world, the actions by one terrorist group such as ISIS can lead to counter reactions and impacts on Muslims in the UK and elsewhere in the world. Nevertheless, a couple of participants pointed out that certain Muslim individuals have failed to condemn these 'trigger' terrorist attacks and therefore they were, to some extent, 'responsible' for the rise in Islamophobic violence.

'There has been an implicit failing in Islam to defend itself. Muslims do not speak out about the wrong things that people do in Islam. There are Muslims like Anjem Choudary who are proverbial thorns in the side of Islam who refuse to condemn the Woolwich attack and the killings committed by ISIS. We are so demonised that we need to explicitly state that we disagree with the actions of ISIS. Unless we do that, people do not know where we agree or not. I am comfortable to speak out against the abhorrent actions of ISIS. These people are doing so much damage to the image of Islam that not to speak out is a bad thing.' (Adam)

Rotherham scandal

Participants also reported that the Rotherham child sexual exploitation scandal had led to a spike in Islamophobic hate crimes, both online and offline. According to British Muslim Youth, a Rotherham-based group launched in 2011, Islamophobic hate crime was at 'unprecedented levels in Rotherham' since the publication of the 2014 Jay Report (which found that 1,400 children suffered sexual exploitation in Rotherham between 1997 and 2013, predominantly by men of Pakistani heritage) (BBC, 2015). Muslim pensioner Mushin Ahmed, aged 81, was on his way to Friday prayers when he was called a 'groomer', kicked and punched to death in August 2015. Participants reported feeling fearful for their lives and described online and offline incidents where they were called 'rapists' and 'paedos' (paedophiles).

'I used to think it was safe to live in Rotherham but now I fear for my life.' (Muhammad)

'I tend to get abuse on Twitter. Typically, I will post something on Twitter and I will then get attacks. Once someone said "all Muslims are paedophiles, rapists" etc and I posted a statistic that showed that 95 per cent of paedophiles are white. But you can't even defend yourself, you are automatically labelled a "Muslim paedophile" yourself.' (Bilal)

'A man commented "What for grooming kids?" below an article I had posted about the conversion of a former warden base into a Muslim community centre.' (Ahmed)

'I live in Rotherham and the grooming case has portrayed all Muslim Pakistani men in Rotherham as paedophiles but what about the Jimmy Saville case? Why did they not mention his religion and colour? This really frustrates me and makes me angry.' (Ibrahim)

'The child sexual abuse scandal in Rotherham and the Trojan Horse investigation at Birmingham schools saw an increase in anti-Muslim attacks at record levels. I was called a "Muslim groomer" by a passer-by while I was giving an interview to BBC radio.' (Hamza)

As the last quote indicates, similarly to the Rotherham scandal, the alleged 'Trojan Horse' scandal in Birmingham framed as a 'jihadist plot' to take over schools had also led to an increase in Islamophobic violence. Nick Clegg, the then deputy prime minister, had written to the general secretary of the Muslim Council of Britain to express his concern that the reporting of the alleged infiltration of Birmingham schools by extremists may have led to a 'deeply regrettable' increase in Islamophobia (Watt, 2014).

Islamophobia and media

Furthermore, participants highlighted the role of media in the 'demonisation' of Muslims. Williams and Burnap (2015) argue that the media play a role in 'setting the agenda', 'transmitting the images' and 'claims making' following 'trigger' events of local, national or international interest. According to Hanes and Machin (2014), if attitudes towards Muslims are influenced by 'trigger' attacks and by media coverage of these attacks, then this finding fits with the proposition of 'attitudinal shocks', where a driver of hate crimes is the level of hatred or bigotry for a particular group in society, which may be influenced by media framing and coverage of attacks. Indeed, there was a consensus view amongst participants of the role of both traditional and social media in promoting Islamophobic hostility, as indicated in the following extracts:

'I experience anti-Muslim hostility from people based on what they read on the *Daily Mail* or what they read on Facebook pages by Britain First.' (Nabeela)

'What you need to know about the Islamophobic agenda is that it is driven by the media. People who look at the media, the news and the papers, they will only believe what the media tells them, and 99 per cent it's negative stories about Islam, so that fuels hate crime towards Muslims.' (Ahmed)

'I blame the media and politicians. The media could explain that the grooming scandal is an individual thing not a Muslim thing but they love to play this game, that it's Islam's fault.' (Ibrahim)

'Islamophobic people are ignorant, close-minded and lack intelligence. I will use a quote by Leo Buscaglia "Only the weak are cruel. Gentleness can only be expected from the strong". I forgive a lot of these ignorant people but I do blame certain sections of media. They are the ones who have grabbed these vulnerable people and it's like telling a child "do not go down there, there is a monster". Those ignorant people who are reading the *Sun* and the *Daily Mail* are like children. They are ignorant, vulnerable individuals.' (Bilal)

'People tend to have these preconceived ideas of Islam. Our media is keen to jump on the bandwagon to emphasise the negative aspects of Islam. If people's first contact with Islam is through the media, then they will automatically think Islam is a terrorist religion. The day Boko Haram attacked a village in Nigeria, they were covered every 15 minutes by the British media. Boko Haram do not have any impact on the UK, yet the media were obsessed with this terrorist group because of their affiliation with Islam. Shortly after the *Charlie Hebdo* shootings, a guy was stabbed to death because he was Muslim and grenades were thrown at a local mosque. There was no coverage of these events but there was constant, graphic coverage of the Paris attacks. I was embarrassed for our media in the sense that it was vulgar.' (Adam)

Relatedly, participants highlighted that people are largely ignorant about the teachings of Islam and that the media do not take sufficient action to educate the public about what 'true' Islam means, as the following extracts illustrate.

'My mother is hostile to my hijab. She watches the news and because of the disproportionate coverage of terrorism she thinks that this is what Islam is.' (Kelly)

'The more Islam is in the media, the more tensions there are. Look at what happened in Paris [*Charlie Hebdo* attacks in January 2015], these attacks are not the teachings of Islam but the media do not promote that. The media thrive on bad stories about Islam, they will not promote stories of good Muslims. They don't give the opportunity to us to show the true image of Islam, they give airtime to idiots like Anjem Choudary. He does not represent Islam, they know that he will say something controversial, that's why they invite him but why not give me an opportunity or someone who is more appropriate to represent Islam?' (Ibrahim)

'Islamophobia is a media-driven picture of Islam that manifests itself in acts of violence towards Muslims. Prior to converting to Islam I was racist and Islamophobic. Ignorance is a big part of Islamophobia.' (Adam)

'Anti-Muslim hate exists because of ignorance about Muslims that is fuelled by the media. People don't understand Muslims because they are not exposed to them. If the only information people get is from the media, then they are naturally going to assume that all Muslims are as bad as ISIS. But if you live next to Mr and Mrs Khan [common Muslim family name] you will realise that Muslims are just normal people.' (Sophie)

Visibility of Islam

In addition to the role of social and traditional media in promoting hostility towards Islam and Muslims, participants also referred to the visibility of Islam as a 'trigger' to online and offline Islamophobic attacks. Indeed, the research literature shows that there is a significant relationship between being 'visible' as a Muslim and experiencing Islamophobic hate crime (Allen et al, 2013; Zempi, 2014). If the markers of Islam are absent, 'passing' as a non-Muslim is possible for those without conspicuous Muslim appearance, and those who do not 'look like' a Muslim. Correspondingly, participants were convinced that it was their distinctive Muslim appearance (such as wearing the Muslim dress for women and the Muslim robe/cap for men) and/or having a Muslim name that made them a target of Islamophobia, as the following quotes indicate.

'The more Muslim you look, the more hostility you will get from people.' (Hamza)

'I am identifiable as a Muslim because I have the full beard, I wear a turban and I also wear the Islamic clothes. I am a very practising Muslim and I feel that is why I am targeted.' (Ibrahim)

'It's like wearing a cone on your head or a flashing light, it's like alert-alert everyone.' (Jasmine)

'In the workplace, if you have a Muslim name you will be discriminated against. The hate that I have experienced over many years is because my name gives away my Muslim identity.' (Bilal)

'My name is Mohammed, the moment they see my name on my passport, that's it. I travel a lot and I always get stopped at airports, I can't understand it. They stop me and nobody else. I was at Heathrow last week, you see officers sitting, doing nothing as people go past but once they see me they get up, ask me to step aside, and question me. Sometimes they check me so thoroughly; they ask me to even take my socks off. I've been to Dubai around 20 times. I feel proud to be Muslim there. I feel proud to be myself there. I feel proud to say "hey my name is Mohammed" and no one will judge me. I can be a Muslim there. It is far easier being a Muslim in Dubai, but I am not leaving the UK, I'm British.' (Mohammed)

Female participants reported feeling particularly vulnerable both online and in the 'real' world because they were visibly identifiable as Muslim women.

'I have a public Twitter account to promote my work and I get regular abuse on that. I have my picture on my Twitter account so they know I am Muslim. I started wearing the hijab two years ago. I was not a Muslim before. I did not get any online or offline abuse at all before wearing the hijab.' (Sophie)

'As a revert, I know that if I chose not to be identifiably Muslim, the abuse would disappear immediately. I reverted to Islam three years ago when I was 40 years old, and within a week I started wearing the hijab and abaya. Prior to wearing the hijab and abaya, I experienced no problems at all. If I were to take off my hijab, and just wear my jeans and t-shirt that I had underneath my abaya, no one would take any notice. I would be as invisible as any other woman on the street.' (Sarah)

'Most victims of Islamophobia are female, there might come a day when we need to send our sisters and daughters back because they are under threat here. I know sisters who have been spat at, or abused, they are more of a target because they are defenceless. They can't fight for themselves.' (Ahmed)

Muslim women are usually seen as the personification of the 'Muslim problem' in the online world. This was evident by the comments used to describe female participants on social media sites, such as a 'national security threat' and comments suggesting that they were forced to wear the veil. In some cases, the hate posts and images contained a number of loaded generalisations with respect to Muslim women as a 'threat' because of their visible identity and affiliation to Islam. Consequently, female participants were more likely to receive abuse than male participants, both online and offline.

> 'We are more vulnerable because we stand out more than the men do. It's partly the woman factor and also the fact that I wear a headscarf. People know that I'm definitely a Muslim. If you are a man with a beard, people are not 100% sure if you are a Muslim.' (Sophie)

This sense of fear and pervading insecurity online was also personified by Kelly, who stated that:

> 'These trolls are not the stereotypical EDL members, they come from all walks of life and all backgrounds, which is alarming. They will set up a hoax ID and from there they can abuse anyone with complete anonymity and hiding behind a false ID.' (Kelly)

Islamophobia as a manifestation of racism and racialisation

It is likely that 'visible' Muslims are particularly vulnerable to abuse on social media. In the online world, individuals who are 'visibly' Muslims have been targeted because they have been identified by their affiliation to Islam (including their name, dress, appearance as well as views, beliefs, comments they have expressed online). In addition to the visibility of their Muslim identity, participants referred to suffering abuse because of their race and ethnicity. In this regard, they described incidents where the nature of the abuse they suffered suggested both

Islamophobic and racist hate crime. Indeed, the literature indicates that race and religion are often interlinked in Islamophobic hate crimes (Meer et al, 2010). Within this framework, the Muslim identity has been subject to a process of racialization, whereby this identity is defined on the basis of the individual's actual or perceived race, rather than exclusively on the basis of their religion. The following quotes indicate participants' experiences of both Islamophobic and racist incidents.

'Anti-Muslim hate crime is tied to racism, and the two cannot be divorced from one another. Many people will say "I am not racist because Islam is not a race", but if the majority of its followers in this country are from an ethnic background, by default they are attacking Muslims on the basis of their race. Actually, nine out of 10 times, the abuse I receive is based on race. Although they use religion because I am identifiable as a Muslim woman, the words that come out of their mouth have to do with race, so race and the religion are tied up together in people's minds.' (Safa)

'I work in the family business supplying fabrics in Luton. I answered the phone to an unhappy customer, Mr Mark Smith. The client complained to me about the fabrics, but when I gave him the option of a refund, Mr Smith asked me what race and religion I belonged to. I stated that I was taken aback by this question and asked Mr Smith what he was implying. Mr Smith said "Your [Muslim] kind come into this country and think you can change it all". Mr Smith continued saying "I know you are a Muslim because there is no one but Muslims in Luton". I told Mr Smith I was baffled by the threats and racist remarks he made.' (Irfan)

Some participants reported that racism has evolved to Islamophobia. While they were growing up in this country they were abused because of their race, whereas in a post 9/11 and 7/7 era they were abused for being Muslim.

> 'Prior to 9/11 and 7/7, the racism I received was because I was brown. Now people accept black and brown people but not Muslims. The EDL have a Sikh division, they will accept everyone except for Muslims. Racism does exist but I don't suffer much abuse for being Pakistani, I suffer abuse for being Muslim.' (Hamza)

> 'I suffered racism as a child growing up in this country. This is something I had to learn to live with and get used to. I've been chased and beaten up as a child by white youth in Sheffield where I grew up. It became normal. Now it's not racism, it's Islamophobia. Racism is on the back burner and Islamophobia is at the forefront.' (Ibrahim)

> 'My grandmother was Jewish, and during World War II people in Liverpool painted swastikas on her front door. This is not the first time that this has happened in this country. It is just that the group haters' new focus is on Muslims. Before it was the Jews, people from Afro-Caribbean countries and the Irish. I am from an Irish background from Liverpool, apart from my grandmother who was Jewish. I used to get comments like "oh you are with the IRA" but now it's like "you are a terrorist".' (Sarah)

Intersectional identities

As indicated above, Islamophobia can be understood as a 'new' form of racism, which can be attributed to Islamophobic attitudes as well as to racist sentiments. Therefore, Islamophobia and racism become mutually reinforcing phenomena. However, this is not to overlook the fact that individuals experience online and offline Islamophobia because their abusers have been motivated either solely or partially by other aspects of their identity, thereby highlighting the notion of 'intersectionality' of identities. As Sallah (2010) points out, intersectionality is a sociological theory postulating that constructed notions of 'difference' impact upon a particular group simultaneously resulting in a cumulative effect. Intersectionality theory explores the ways in which systems of oppression such as racism, sexism and homophobia simultaneously structure social relations (Collins, 2000). Intersectionality theory posits that systems of oppression should be understood as an interlocking web of mutually reinforcing power structures, each of which depends on the others; rather than hierarchically ranking systems of oppression, each system operates in different yet overlapping ways (Collins, 2000; Crenshaw, 1991). From this perspective, intersectionality can be understood as a nexus of identities that work together to render certain individuals as 'ideal' targets to attack, especially in the minds of their abusers (Yuval-Davis, 2011). Accordingly, the following quote illustrates the intersectionality amongst race, religion and gender. "I suffer abuse because I am not just a Muslim woman wearing the hijab. I am also a coloured person (Aisha)."

The research findings show that there is considerable intersectionality amongst religion, race/ethnicity and gender. For example, participants pointed out that being a convert to Islam, rendered them particularly vulnerable to both online and offline abuse, as the following quotes demonstrate.

'I get nasty tweets, pms, Facebook messages saying how I am a "race traitor".' (Jasmine)

'When I converted to Islam, many of my friends who were previously my friends stopped being my friends, not through my personal choice but because they didn't treat me the same after.' (Adam)

'People will message me [on Facebook] and try to start arguments, for example, a troll messaged me to say that "we are all a bunch of terrorists, and that we have been brainwashed to convert to Islam".' (Sarah)

As this discussion illustrates, the 'visibility' and intersectionality of victims' identities also emerge as contributing factors to manifestations of Islamophobia, both online and offline.

NATURE AND EXTENT OF ONLINE AND OFFLINE ISLAMOPHOBIA

The terrorist attacks in Paris, Tunisia and Woolwich have led to a significant increase in Islamophobic hostility, which has culminated in a rise in reprisal attacks against Muslim communities. Typically, these attacks happen in street-based Islamophobic hostility; nevertheless, an increase in online Islamophobia has resulted in a debate about the nature of online and offline Islamophobia, and the relationship between the two. Muslims, particularly those with a 'visible' Muslim identity, suffer Islamophobic intimidation, abuse and threats of violence both online and offline. Thus, for victims, whether 'visibly' Muslim or not, it is difficult to isolate the online threats from the intimidation, violence and abuse that they suffer offline. Rather, there is a continuity of Islamophobic hostility in both the cyber and in the 'real' world. Against this background, this chapter discusses the nature of online and offline anti-Muslim hostility.

Online Islamophobic hostility

In a post 9/11 and 7/7 climate, Islamophobic hostility has increased significantly (Weller et al., 2001; Commission on British Muslims and Islamophobia, 2004; McGhee, 2005; Githens-Mazer and Lambert, 2010). In 2013, Tell MAMA found that 74 per cent of online Islamophobic incidents had been reported to them (Feldman et al., 2013). A steady increase in Islamophobic hostility is further reinforced by data that shows that between May 2013 and February 2014, there were 734 reported cases of Islamophobic abuse, and of these, 599 were incidents of online abuse and threats, while the others were offline attacks such as violence, threats and assaults (Lancashire Telegraph, 2014).

The murder of Lee Rigby in Woolwich in May 2013 and the terrorist attacks in Paris and Tunisia in 2015, the actions of ISIS and wider international and regional events, have fuelled the growth of Islamophobic hostility on social media, as well as in the streets of Britain. For example, the recent Rotherham child sexual exploitation scandal in the UK and the activities of Islamic State militants, such as the murder of British aid worker David Haines in September 2014, have perpetuated Islamophobic sentiments and 'legitimised' Islamophobic attacks both online and offline (Dodd and Williams, 2014). For example, after the Paris shooting in January 2015, the #KillAllMuslims hashtag was 'trending' in the UK and was accompanied by a number of direct threats made targeting Muslim communities such as 'blowing up a mosque' and 'shooting a Muslim for fun'.

Cyber hate is a complex phenomenon and is used to promote an ideology that incites violence, racial hatred, intolerance and allows hate groups to exert cyber power and social control. Indeed, the profile of these online offenders seems to have been formed from those seeking and searching for an 'identity', which allows them to use and exploit social and political beliefs as an ideology which has no respect for the individuals or groups it targets (Tajfel, 1970; McKenna and Bargh, 1998; Prince, 2012). This therefore can result in them trying to use online methods as a means of self-protectionism and false patriotism, such as far-right groups (see the English Defence League and Britain First), which are apt at fuelling Islamophobic hostility.

This is often played out by threatening, abusive and coordinated online messages through the use of sites like Facebook and Twitter, which promote messages of racial hatred (Awan, 2016). Moreover, they are not confined to social networking sites but include blogging sites, online chat rooms, and other virtual platforms, which have been used to promote online Islamophobic hatred, often in the form of racist jokes and stereotypical 'banter'. The danger is this that when these incidents go unchecked, this type of online abuse can also lead to the normalisation of such behaviour and even an escalation to physical attacks (Allport, 1954).

Our study found that Islamophobic hate crime has increased online particularly against Muslim women, for example, via social networking sites such as Facebook, Twitter and Instagram (see also Awan, 2014). In a study conducted by Sheridan (2006: 319), which examined online Islamophobic abuse, it emerged that, 'Explicitly Islamophobic content was observed on the Internet and via emails and text messages, as well as via more traditional hate crime methods such as abusive telephone calls, messages left on cars, and anonymous mail sent to private homes, mosques, and Islamic cultural centers'. Within this context, the images, and posts in particular, contained a number of stereotypes with respect to Muslim women and wider Muslim communities. Muslim women were therefore often living in a sense of fear and having to monitor their protection online. One of our participants, Hira, a White British convert who wears the hijab and abaya, mainly uses Facebook but has had to make her online profile private, because of the consistent online Islamophobic abuse she has suffered. She noted that, "I've had to re-adjust all my security settings, so that only friends can contact me or see my profile because of the abuse I've suffered". Similar types of hostility arose when Muslim women began publicly making statements or expressing their opinions; they were confronted with abuse, misogynistic comments and threats of violence.

> 'I've suffered a lot of Islamophobic comments on Facebook and Twitter. When I write an article or share my opinions online, people usually reply with horrible Islamophobic comments. If you are a Muslim on social media, you are prone to receive abuse.' (Aisha)

Furthermore, Halima has also been the victim of the vitriolic hate espoused by some members of the EDL and reported the online abuse she suffered to the police because of the nature of the direct threats made against her. Below is one example where Halima was targeted on Twitter. "Hahahhahaa I told you my agenda hunny. Don't worry I will knock you out" (Halima).

For Halima, these threatening messages also included online verbal hostility and images used where she was targeted because of her visible 'identity' as a Muslim. Online abuse and intimidation can often have devastating consequences that are difficult to remove and can cause a lot of damage when images, videos and pictures are used to target individuals. For example, Halima had her picture tweeted, with the accompanying text: 'You Burqa wearing slut.' As noted above, the use of pictures can magnify the abuse and hostility online leading to serious consequences for the victims. For example, Amin has also suffered similar online Islamophobic abuse. In his case, an image was used of him with the caption 'suspended child grooming taxi drivers', despite the post being false and malicious. Fatima, has also suffered online abuse. After publishing an article on her Twitter account, she was targeted online by someone who said: 'Go f*** yourself, go f*** a goat you Islamic extremist piece of SHIT!' She added that "I was called a Muzlamic and I needed sense f***king into me." Fatima did not feel confident enough to report this incident to the police, because of fear she would not be taken seriously.

The above examples show that online comments are contributing towards the stigmatisation and the 'othering' of Muslim communities who are now being treated as official 'suspects'. Both offline and online incidents can also have a similar pattern and a trend, which is based primarily on the perpetrator inciting violence and posing real offline threats against Muslim communities (Yar, 2013). The above incidents show that online hate crime committed against Muslim communities can have a detrimental impact upon the government community cohesion strategy as well as a more personal impact on the victims and the families affected by such measures.

Street-based Islamophobic hostility

For the purposes of street-based Islamophobia, two distinct categories emerged from our findings where (a) Muslims are stereotyped, demonised and dehumanised; and (b) calls are made for specific violence against Muslims. These two factors are discussed in more detail below.

Stereotypes, demonisation and dehumanisation of Muslims

Whilst online stereotypes were used to depict Muslims in a negative manner, in the online world, such effects were used to characterise Muslims and particularly Muslim women in a negative way with strong verbal and physical abuse noted. Indeed, evidence suggests that veiled Muslim women are at heightened risk of Islamophobic hostility in public by virtue of their visible 'Muslimness' (Allen and Nielsen, 2002; Allen, 2010; Githens-Mazer and Lambert, 2010; Zempi, 2014). Popular perceptions that veiled Muslim women are passive, oppressed and powerless increase their chance of assault, thereby marking them as an 'easy' target to attack. Zempi (2014) conducted 60 individual and 20 focus group interviews with veiled Muslim women in mosques, Muslim schools, Islamic centres, and Muslim homes, and found that they were persistent and multiple victims of Islamophobic hate crime in public. Whilst suffering manifestations of Islamophobic hostility in public, some participants had also suffered persistent online abuse such as name-calling, online threats to physically harm, online stalking and sexual harassment (Zempi, 2014). Participants referred to such incidents as 'part and parcel' of their everyday lives.

Along similar lines, participants in the present study described suffering abuse on a daily basis. Hira noted that "As soon as I became identifiably Muslim, I got nasty looks, threats and abuse, and that's an everyday experience, especially because I am a white British Muslim." A number of other participants had also experienced abuse because of their visible identification as being Muslim. For example, Mohammad talked about how his children have been targeted by Islamophobic abuse in schools.

> 'I've had many problems at my children's school. Being Muslim creates a lot of problems for them. If my child is bullied or attacked, teachers will ignore it. Other pupils call them names like "paki get lost", swearing, "go back home", "you don't belong here", "Muslim monkeys", other pupils have pulled their headscarves. This has happened many times to all of my children. There are double standards for my children because they're Muslim.' (Mohammad)

Moreover, the issue of Islamophobic bullying was consistent with a wider problem of institutional levels of Islamophobia in the workplace, as indicated in the following quote.

> 'I've suffered racism and Islamophobia in the workplace. I was once in a board meeting and someone called Islam a "terrorist religion". People judge me by my Muslim name and the colour of my skin. I've been to board meetings where I got a certain look. It's only when I start talking that people take me seriously.' (Bilal)

Mythen et al (2009: 744) state that 'Forms of collective victimisation were perceived to pertain more to discrimination enacted by institutions on Muslims as a group. In this vein, our participants discussed counter-terrorism measures, foreign policy, policing, the criminal justice system, education and the media. Although we define these forms of victimisation separately for analytical purposes, it is important to point out that they are – and were articulated as – in interchange. This symbiosis of the individual and the collective is critical in grasping expressed victimisation amongst the Pakistani Britons whom we engaged with'.

One of our participants, Jasmine, who wears a hijab, stated that "I have received racist abuse, which was not relevant to me. People are constantly asking me 'Where are you from, where are you really from?' They can't comprehend the fact that I could be white British, born here, and actually a Muslim who wears the hijab". Verbal abuse also impacted upon Hamza who has had people calling him names. This level of abuse meant Hamza made the choice not to wear any clothing that would make him visibly stand out as Muslim because of the fear he would be targeted with further Islamophobic hostility.

> 'I do wear Muslim clothes occasionally, for example, when I go to the mosque but in general I don't, mainly for political reasons. If I were to wear it, it would create further division. People already see Muslims as different. I know I will suffer hostility for wearing it so I don't wear it. I don't look like a Muslim 100 per cent because I don't wear it all the time but I do have a beard so people realise I'm a Muslim.' (Hamza)

Mohammad also stated that 'My postman would not deliver my post because I am Muslim. I complained to the local media, they spoke to the post office's management and they sorted it out. Now I get my mail from another postman, the other one has moved to another area'. Our research found that such notions create a polarisation and a 'them versus us narrative', which is often used to stereotype Muslims as being dangerous and a security risk. This was personified by many participants who felt they were unfairly labelled as 'extremists', 'fanatics' and 'radicals'. This was also reinforced by how Muslims would be viewed in their ordinary day to day lives. For example, Bilal stated that:

> 'A few years ago, I went into a shop to buy shoes for my 82-year-old mother. I went into the shop as an adult, and as a chartered psychologist, as a British citizen, dressed in professional clothes, and the lady behind the counter refused to serve me. I said "Hey I am standing here, why are you not serving me?" She totally ignored me; she walked away from the counter and went towards the stock room.' (Bilal)

Another disturbing account of Islamophobic hostility was experienced by Faisal.

Case study 2: Faisal, 49 years old, Pakistani

Faisal, would pray in a shed outside the food store in Liverpool where he worked as a security guard, leaving the door of the shed wide open. On one occasion, Faisal reported how the assistant manager went outside and locked the door of the shed as she passed by. As this door cannot be opened from the inside, Faisal continuously banged on the door but had no response. He then called the shop, at which point the assistant manager answered the phone and he asked her to open the door. She did so and said that she could not hear the banging. He maintained that there is no way that she did not see him in the shed as the door was left wide open. Faisal stated that "They threatened me and said go back to your own country you are Osama Bin Laden". He added that: "They used foul language against me, they snatched my phone and were very aggressive towards me. They really bullied me and told me to go home and they don't want me."

In another case of offline Islamophobia, Hira who wears the hijab, was on the train when a group of white men began verbally and physically abusing her. In her case, the perpetrators kept waving alcoholic drinks and an unknown substance in her face and asking her if she wanted some, and also asking her if she 'eats bacon' or if she has 'a bomb under her scarf?' This continued with a chant, "We are racist, we are racist and we love it". They also started shouting "Do it with the nun, it's better than having none" and continued to point at her and ridicule her. Hira stated that:

'One of them tried to speak to me but I gave him the silent treatment and then they started chanting "Do it with the nun, it's better than having none". I asked the person abusing me to stop but he wouldn't. Then they dropped alcohol on my coat.' (Hira)

Calls for physical violence against Muslims

As indicated in the following quotes, a number of participants also spoke about the disturbing nature of abuse they had suffered as a result of Islamophobia.

'My wife [wears the niqab] was standing at a bus stop in the city centre when a White British male approached her, looked her up and down and said "you fucking scum". My wife was completely shocked. She is used to people being condescending and rolling their eyes at her, frowning or heavily sighing, but she has never experienced this level of aggression before.' (Bilal)

'I don't have a beard but when I wear Muslim clothes I can be identified as a Muslim. I'm proud to be a British Muslim but I suffer a lot of Islamophobia, especially at weekends. I work in a taxi office in the weekends, and I suffer a lot of abuse fuelled by drunken behaviour by clients.' (Ahmed)

'There are two types of Islamophobia. One type is when people will definitely make a nasty comment and they'll say it to your face. The other type is more insidious; they will not say it to your face but they are Islamophobic deep down inside although they will not show it. If you're applying for a job, they will discriminate against you. The second type of Islamophobia is much more difficult to prove.' (Ibrahim)

'I've had problems from my neighbours. When I moved in, they wrote racist slogans on the walls of my house, they threw a brick at the window, they broke my car.' (Mohammad)

'I was on maternity ward and this patient was in labour, when she saw me with my hijab she swore at me. She said "I don't want my baby to see your terrorist face. I don't want my child to come to this world and see someone like you a terrorist. Leave my country. How dare, you come to my ward and show your ugly face". I then left my job as a midwife.' (Asma)

Padela and Heisler's (2010) study assessed the discrimination faced by Arab American Muslims after September 11, 2001. They found that 25 per cent of the respondents reported post September 11 personal or familial abuse, and 15 per cent reported that they personally had a bad experience related to their ethnicity and this level of abuse was associated with higher levels of psychological distress, lower levels of happiness and worse health status. Padela and Heisler (2010: 284) state that 'Personal bad experiences related to ethnicity were associated with increased psychological distress and reduced happiness. Perceptions of not being respected within US society, and greater reported effects of September 11 with respect to personal security and safety, were associated with higher levels of psychological distress'.

We argue that such behaviour can become normalised by offenders who use it to target and call for violent action against Muslim communities. For example, Safa who wears the hijab stated that she had been called "F****ing Pakis, F***ing Slag, let's blow your face off." Safa added that the name calling did not stop there and included physical violence. She stated that "It didn't stop her from slapping me against my face, pulling my headscarf and kicking me on the left side on my hips". Like most victims of hate crime, Safa felt too scared to report the incident to the police. She told us "I was scared to report it initially, but when I did, the police response was so poor and I felt humiliated even though someone had threatened to blow my face off".

Zarah also experienced similar threats of physical violence. In her case, the offender told her that he wanted to "...smash this down on your head and he made me feel frightened and fearful". Whilst many of the female participants were victims of abuse, whereby perpetrators pulled their hijab and/or spat at them, for male participants this included people pulling their beards. For example, Faisal cited examples of when past line managers expressed concerns about his appearance, as well as instances where customers had pulled his beard and subjected him to racist and Islamophobic comments. He added, "It has been tough".

On another occasion, Mrs Faisal was driving their children to school and found a parking space opposite an elderly care home and indicated to park. The perpetrator appeared behind them, and continuously honked her car horn at her and then aggressively overtook her. While she was overtaking, she held up her middle finger at them. Once they parked the car, the perpetrator began calling them 'F****** Pakis'. Then when Mrs Faisal put her hand out to signal her to calm down, the lady slapped her hand and then pushed her twice in the chest. Mrs Faisal is a heart patient and immediately started gasping. She then moved away with her children and called the police. While she was on the phone to the police, the perpetrator continued to scream at Mrs Faisal. The police noted everything and urged Mrs Faisal to leave the scene.

In Nabeela's case, she stated that "A man ran up to me in and spat in my face twice because I am Muslim. He accused me and my people in the Middle East of "killing Christians"'. For Hira, the man in the seat next to her poked her ribs and shoulder a couple of times, and Asma had also witnessed physical aggression and violence towards her. Asma stated that "I was in a Halal KFC shop and someone came behind me and removed my headscarf in this queue". Clearly, for a number of participants, there was an increase in feelings of insecurity both online and offline with many participants voicing and expressing concerns about this. These feelings of insecurity are heightened when victims have suffered multiple incidents of Islamophobic hate crime, as it impacts upon their overall confidence and the levels of fear they have.

'I was waiting for the bus and someone pulled my hijab but no one stepped in.' (Jasmine)

'I travel a lot for my work, I work for a multinational company. Last time I was at Heathrow airport, I got accused of using a false passport. I always get a random unannounced security check at Heathrow every single time. I feel safe if I am within the Masjid but going anywhere else can be a problem.' (Sarah)

The nature of online and offline Islamophobia varies in the manner in which people are targeted. Although those means may be different, the aims are the same. Muslims that are visibly identifiable because of their appearance are more likely to be targeted. In the online world, female participants were targeted most through vitriolic, misogynistic and racist abuse. In the offline world, female participants were also likely to be pushed, spat at, verbally assaulted and physically abused. For Muslim men, in the offline world, encounters of institutional levels of Islamophobia existed and led to a rise in overall levels of fear, insecurity and confidence. This included examples of Muslim men being targeted in the workplace and having to pray outside in a garden shed for fear that they would be vilified. These levels of frustration and anger are likely to impact upon victims of Islamophobic hate crime and discussed in more detail in the next chapter. One of the key factors that emerged from these case studies is the fact that many of the participants did not report the incidents of Islamophobic hostility to the police. This was mainly because victims felt they would not be taken seriously and also had an overall lack of confidence within the police service and the wider criminal justice system. Such incidents and a lack of reporting can have tremendous implications for how social media companies and the police tackle online and offline Islamophobia. If victims of Islamophobia, both online and offline are to be taken seriously then there is an urgent need to help victims have confidence in the police service though building trust.

IMPACTS OF ONLINE AND OFFLINE ISLAMOPHOBIA

This chapter discusses the impacts of online and offline Islamophobic hate crime for victims and their families. Correspondingly, participants experienced a range of psychological and emotional responses such as low confidence, depression and anxiety as well as increased feelings of vulnerability, fear and insecurity. Additionally, participants highlighted the relationship between online and offline Islamophobia, and described living in fear because of the possibility of online threats materialising in the 'real' world. Many participants reported taking steps to become less 'visibly' Muslim – for example by taking the veil off for women and shaving their beards for men, or having a western name – in order to protect themselves from future abuse.

Emotional and psychological impacts

Generally speaking, crime can incur a number of different 'costs' following a victimisation experience such as psychological, emotional, physical and financial implications. However, research shows that hate crime has specific psychological effects upon victims (McDevitt et al, 2001; Herek et al, 2002). In this regard, hate crime often contributes to symptoms associated with post-traumatic stress disorder (PTSD), such as anxiety, anger and despair (Otis and Skinner, 1996; Herek et al, 2002). Studies indicate that hate crime 'hurts more' than other forms of crime on the basis that hate crime is more damaging and traumatic for victims than other types of crime (Iganski, 2001). Specifically, hate crime studies highlight the more severe impact for victims of hate crime when compared to non-hate victims (see, for example, Smith et al, 2012; Chakraborti et al, 2014; Williams and Tregidga, 2014).

Our participants reported experiencing a range of psychological and emotional responses to online and offline Islamophobia such as guilt, anger, fear, sadness, low confidence, isolation and helplessness. Given that they were targeted because of the 'visibility' of their Muslim identity – which was easily identifiable because of their Muslim name and/or Muslim appearance either online or offline – participants were unable to take comfort in the belief that what happened to them was simply random and 'could have happened to anyone'. Rather, they were forced to view this abuse as an attack on their Muslim identity. Some participants reported feeling weak, helpless and powerless because they felt that they were not 'allowed' to challenge Islamophobia, as the following extracts indicate:

'When incidents like the Charlie Hebdo happen, I am asked to condemn it and I do condemn it, not only as a Muslim but also as a human being, but when attacks against Muslims happen, no one asks me to condemn it. That is Islamophobia for me and it is very upsetting. Attacks like the Charlie Hebdo are un-Islamic, inhumane and completely unacceptable but I am offended, I don't see how I, as an individual who already suffers Islamophobia, need to accept such cartoons that insult our Prophet, who we will love more than anybody else. People don't understand why we are offended. It's like we are not allowed to be offended. If I said I am offended, I would suffer more Islamophobia. That's why we stay quiet. We condemn the killings but we stay quiet about speaking out against Islamophobia. We are not allowed to speak out. I don't support the killings, but I don't support the cartoons either. We feel helpless.' (Hamza)

'What can we do? We are powerless. We need to find a solution to the Islamophobia we are facing at the moment.' (Ibrahim)

Throughout interviews, a key finding was that offline Islamophobic hate attacks increased feelings of fear, insecurity and anxiety amongst all participants, as indicated in the following quotes.

'I used to wear a hijab when I was younger but now I'm wary of wearing it because I'm too scared.' (Halima)

'I do get scared, anything can happen to me. I do fear for my life sometimes.' (Aisha)

'It is scary because we are constantly under attack.' (Ahmed)

'Members of the EDL defaced the local mosque with dog poo and a pig's head. There's a big presence of EDL members living in the local community. I feel very scared for me and my family.' (Adam)

As a result, some participants were reluctant to leave the house, especially on their own because of fear of being attacked, as the following quotes demonstrate.

'We stay in, we don't go out because we are scared of what will happen. If I leave the house I am usually accompanied by my husband or my son.' (Nabeela)

'My wife wears the niqab and she had many incidents where people have made nasty remarks, so just to avoid conflict we don't go out.' (Ibrahim)

At the same time, online Islamophobic hate crimes made participants particularly fearful due to the anonymity that the internet provides its users. The internet allows people to take on a new and/or anonymous identity, and to bypass traditional editorial controls, to share their views with millions. Online Islamophobic hate messages can be sent anonymously or by using a false identity, making it extremely difficult to identify the offender. The anonymity aspect in cases of online Islamophobic hate abuse is extremely frightening as the perpetrator could be anyone.

'I am scared because in face-to-face situations I can see who the perpetrator is but when someone does it online I always think who is it? Who is hiding behind the keyboard sending me messages of hate?' (Aisha)

Online abuse materialising in the 'real' world

Participants argued that it was often difficult to isolate online threats from the intimidation, violence and abuse that they suffer in the 'real' world. Instead, they described a continuity of Islamophobic hostility both online and offline, particularly in the globalised world. Specifically, participants reported living in fear because of the possibility of online threats materialising in the 'real' world, as demonstrated in the following quotes.

'I am scared, I fear for my life because at the end of the day they [cyber perpetrators] might come and find me because my Twitter profile is public.' (Aisha)

'I know many Muslims who have been physically attacked and verbally attacked. Personally, I have been called "Muslim scum", "jihadist" and "paedophile". I have been bullied and slandered on a forum online. People call Prophet Mohammad a "paedophile", and they often say to me that "we [Muslims] believe in a paedophile". There is a popular misconception that one of Prophet Mohammad's wives was a child bride. By association, I have been called a "paedophile". This was online, they were so nasty and horrible towards me that I did feel fearful to the point I thought that they would turn up at my house, and hurt me and my family because they knew who I was and where I lived.' (Adam)

There is a strong relationship between online and offline Islamophobic hate crime on the basis that online threats can escalate into the 'real' world, especially when the identity of the potential victim is known. For example, Zarah, who is a high-profile convert to Islam working in the media, recalls experiencing online Islamophobic abuse whereby the perpetrators threatened her as they knew where she lived, and her identity was well known because of her occupation both in social and traditional media.

'I have received telephone calls after converting to Islam with direct threats made offline as well as online via social media platforms, such as Twitter. In one particular incident someone said "We know who you are and where you live".' (Zarah)

For some participants, online Islamophobic hate crime had effects in the 'real' world. For example, in the case of Amin, an image was used of him on Twitter with the caption 'suspended child grooming taxi drivers' despite the post being false and malicious.

'They used a picture of me on Twitter and said 'taxi driver groomer suspended'. I can't even get a job in Rotherham now because of this picture although I was not involved in the Rotherham scandal. Rotherham is a small town and people get to know things quickly. I reported it to the police but they weren't interested. They should have protected me but they didn't.' (Amin)

The case of Amin directly shows the link between online and offline Islamophobia on the basis that he could not find a job because of the fact that his reputation was damaged online. He reported feeling uncomfortable walking down the streets in Rotherham because people might recognise his picture from Twitter, and believe that he was one of the perpetrators of the grooming scandal. This could put his safety at risk in the 'real' world. Clearly, online hate messages and comments contribute towards the stigmatisation and the 'othering' of Muslims in the 'real' world. This demonstrates that in reality, the boundaries between online and offline Islamophobic hate crime may be more blurred than the terms imply.

Responses to repeat victimisation

Collectively, repeat incidents of online and offline Islamophobia increased feelings of insecurity, vulnerability and anxiety amongst our participants. Bowling (2009) states that repeated or persistent victimisation can undermine the security of actual and potential victims, and induce fear and anxiety. As a result, participants reported feeling extremely vulnerable for themselves and they were also concerned about the safely of their family. For example, Ibrahim expressed his fear for the safety of his wife who wears the niqab, whilst Mohammad argued that he did not challenge perpetrators when his children were with him as he feared for their safety.

'My wife is very vulnerable when she is on her own. I fear for her safety.' (Ibrahim)

'I have been called "Muslim terrorist", "Here's come Osama Bin Laden". Normally I answer back, but if my children are with me I ignore it.' (Mohammad)

In light of the above, participants emphasised that they always had to keep their guard up and be vigilant. As such, they felt anxious and were constantly on the alert, especially in public spaces. Anxiety was usually expressed as excessive fear and worry, which was often coupled with feelings of tension, restlessness and vigilance.

'You might find it bizarre but when I walk on the street I am always watching out in case anything happens. I am a big guy, six feet tall, I stand out as a sore thumb. Sometimes people look at me with disgust.' (Ibrahim)

'It has made me feel uncomfortable and always looking over my shoulder.' (Fatima)

At the same time though, it is important to recognise that the continual threat of online and offline Islamophobic abuse can be emotionally draining for victims who feel the need to be constantly on the alert, even to the extent that they might become paranoid, as the following extracts illustrate.

'To be honest, I have slowed down with my openness on Twitter because I feel very unsafe, I feel very vulnerable. There was a time I felt so vulnerable just being in the UK because of my Twitter account. I became paranoid, that everybody might be watching me, the government, people, everyone really.' (Bilal)

'The only thing that the government is after is intelligence. There is a lot of spying going on at the moment with all the ISIS stuff in the news. We are not trusted, we are left to deal with problems on our own, and then we are blamed for everything. The way it's going it's like Muslims and Islam are responsible for everything when actually they are looking for someone to blame. They feel threatened by us because of the Islamic lifestyle. They want us to become like them.' (Aisha)

Relatedly, case Study 3 highlights Safa's feelings of weakness and helplessness after being physically attacked by a group of white girls in Manchester.

Case study 3: Safa, 19 years old, British Libyan

I was involved in a racist attack which included my scarf getting pulled off and my friend being called 'a f****** p*** slag'. Me and my friend were in Piccadilly Gardens drinking hot chocolate and catching up about work/uni as you do. A hijabi beggar came to a group of white girls (that were sat next to us), having her hand out asking for money and they replied by swearing at her and saying 'Why are you begging in my country, go back to your own county. What if I went to your country and begged for money I would get kidnapped and killed'. I overheard what these girls were saying and to be honest I couldn't keep quiet. I spoke to the girls politely and said "Listen that wasn't a nice thing to say". They lashed out at me and started swearing, they said 'go back to your country you f****** terrorist p***, we will bomb your face off'. They then slapped me, pulled my headscarf and kicked me on the left side on my hips. That didn't hurt me. What hurt me was what they said. The words hit me more than the physical attack. You know when you hear these things being said and you get really upset that people are saying these things, but try having someone screaming it to your face. I felt weak. I felt horrible and from the shock I started crying. Maybe it wasn't my business because I knew I was getting myself into trouble, but then I thought if I don't stand up against these people, who will? How will they ever learn? I can't keep seeing people get abused. It was a disgusting scene and I hope, I really hope that no one ever goes through this. I did go to the police station and filled a report and a statement, and they said that there's only 0.1 per cent chance that they will find these girls but I feel I did the right thing.

Islamic identity

Furthermore, a couple of participants felt that Islamophobic hate crime experiences made their faith in Islam stronger. In this regard, Islam became a more salient and important marker of identity in response to experiences of online and/or offline Islamophobia. Such experiences increased in-group solidarity and identification with their religious identity. Brown (2001) observes that as Muslim identities have been constructed as 'other' to western identities, an attempt to distort Muslim identities, or to suppress the symbols of these identities, often has the opposite effect; it strengthens these identities. As the following quotes illustrate, suffering Islamophobic hate crime made some participants more determined to continue to practise Islam.

'Islamophobia has pushed me closer to practising Islam. I am more passionate now about my Muslim identity. I feel I don't belong anywhere else.' (Bilal)

'I was walking to the shops, a man came behind me, pulled my hijab and strangled me. No one stood up for me and he said to me "Are you going to bomb Boots?" I didn't want to take the case to court or tell the police, instead I just read the Quran. I love my hijab more when they attack me for it.' (Asma)

Furthermore, some participants commented on the links between suffering Islamophobia and becoming radicalised. They highlighted the risks of radicalisation especially for young people who have suffered repeat and persistent online and/or offline Islamophobic hate crimes, as the following quote illustrates.

'Islamophobia has affected Muslims. This is why Muslims are going to Syria. This is why they support ISIS. When people experience Islamophobic abuse, they will be easily radicalised. They feel weak, lonely, isolated and rejected from British society. This is when these hate preachers pick them up and brainwash them. If you are victimised, you are weak. Jihadi John and others who support ISIS were vulnerable. Vulnerability is the number one factor why Muslims go to Syria. These young people are groomed to go to Syria, groomed to become terrorists, groomed to blow themselves up.' (Hamza)

Moreover, some participants reported feeling angry, upset and frustrated because they were targeted for being Muslim. Indeed, hate crime studies show both specific and generalised frustration and anger on the part of victims – towards the perpetrator and towards a culture of bias and exclusion (Williams and Tregidga, 2014).

'It upsets me because Muslims have contributed a lot in this country and we continue to contribute to the economy and to all aspects of life but we are not trusted by the government, the police and the media. It upsets me that Muslims are to blame for everything. There are other communities that have worse problems than us. Without stereotyping or being prejudiced, the white community have their own problems. They have the highest rate of teenage pregnancy in Europe. Are we responsible for that as well?' (Ahmed)

'It's not only the sniggers, the pointing, the name calling, it's also the way I am treated by shop assistants and it's just because I wear a piece of cloth on my head. I know that if I walked out of the shop, changed my clothes, went in again, the shop assistant would have been all smiles. It's unfair to be treated not based on who you are but on what you look like. It makes me feel upset and angry.' (Nabeela)

'I suffer Islamophobia all the time. People have labelled me as a "p*** bomber" just by looking at me, which makes me very angry. I feel I have to pay for something that it is not even my fault.' (Bilal)

'These men started sending me vile messages, they said "I was talking shit". It was quite a few messages that I received. I tried to respond by giving a comment but that just inflamed the situation and the next two days I spotted one of them. I was so angry that I confronted him.' (Fatima)

'My daughter is running a blog. People do latch on and she receives unpleasant tweets, people online ask her "What is it like having a mom who supports a violent ideology?" She is still a Christian and has met my Muslim friends. When the racists or hard line secularists attack her she gets upset.' (Zarah)

Also, affective responses that were common amongst our participants were isolation, withdrawal, loneliness, depression and a sense of rejection from wider society. Islamophobic hate crime has long-lasting effects for victims including making them afraid to engage with other communities and feeling like social outcasts, as indicated in the following quotes.

'I feel very isolated and I have become quite cynical about non-Muslims.' (Hafsa)

'Suffering Islamophobia has made me become insular, lack confidence, I feel I am not accepted.' (Bilal)

'My eldest son was studying aeronautical engineering in his second year. He went for a job and they told him "Why do you want to study aeronautics? Is it because you want to blow up a plane?" He has now left his studies. This is our home, we don't want to leave this country but where do we belong?' (Asma)

This discussion shows that participants were multiple and repeat victims of both online and offline Islamophobia. Rarely did participants describe Islamophobic hate crime/incidents as 'one-off'; rather, there was always the sense, the fear, the expectation for another attack. From this perspective, manifestations of Islamophobia were perceived as 'normal'. The fact that Islamophobic hate crime was seen as a normative part of their lived experiences also meant that some participants had become 'used to it' and in some cases 'immune' to it, as the following quotes indicate.

'I have been called a "Muslim terrorist" so many times but I have grown a thicker skin as a result.' (Bilal)

'I am not afraid anymore because I am so used to it. I have to live here so I need to adjust myself to the abuse. If I beat the crap out of them I will be in trouble. I take the abuse and keep my head down. I just want to carry on with my life.' (Muhammad)

'In a way, I anticipate it to happen so I am not scared. For example, when people are pointing at me from far, I expect them to say or do something when I'm close. It is scary when people have spat at me or pulled my headscarf and I did not see that coming.' (Sophie)

'We can't say anything. If we say anything we are going to make it worse. What do you say to people who abuse you but they do not know who you are, they have never spoken to you, they don't even know your name. The fact that we are Muslims is enough to make them hate and intimidate us. I've accepted Islamophobia. We have suffered so much Islamophobic abuse from politicians, media, people on the street, people on social media that we don't know what Islamophobia is any more. Islamophobia is legitimised. The things you can say for the Muslim community and get away with, you can't say for any other community.' (Irfan)

'When I suffer abuse in public, people walk off or stare. It is normal. If I were in the Muslim community, it would be a different story, people would step in.' (Sarah)

Becoming 'less visible'

Ultimately, the threat of both online and offline Islamophobia had 'forced' some participants to change their lifestyle and/or take steps to become less 'visibly' Muslim. For instance, some participants who had converted to Islam (such as Sarah, Kelly, Sophie and Adam) explained that they kept their English name to avoid suffering Islamophobic hostility. Other participants who were born into Islam had adopted western names in order to hide their Muslim identity, especially in the online world. Zempi (2014) found that veiled Muslim women often tried to become less 'visible' and thus less vulnerable by taking the veil off. Similarly, our participants revealed downplaying their 'Muslimness' by taking the hijab or niqab off, or by dressing in western clothes, as the following extracts illustrate.

> 'I do not feel safe to wear the hijab up in my hometown because of the dangers there. I take my hijab and abaya off when I go to my hometown because of the abuse I will get as a result.' (Sarah)

> 'I do get funny looks on the street because of my beard. When I dress in more traditionally Islamic clothing, for example, when I go to the mosque, I get more insulting, derogatory comments. It makes life easier when I dress in western clothes.' (Adam)

> 'I do wear Muslim clothes occasionally, for example, when I go to the mosque, but in general I don't, mainly for political reasons. If I were to wear it, it would create further division. People already see Muslims as different. I know I will suffer hostility for wearing it so I don't wear it. I don't look like a Muslim 100% because I don't wear it all the time but I do have a beard so people realise I'm a Muslim.' (Hamza)

The constant threat of Islamophobic hate crime had forced participants to adopt a siege mentality and keep a low profile in order to reduce the potential for future attacks. Some participants attempted to manage impressions of their Muslim identity in the online and/or offline world mainly through concealment with the aim to reduce the risk of future abuse. Perry and Alvi (2012) state that this is not a voluntary choice, but the 'safe' choice. Whether in the online or 'real' world, Islamophobic hate crime creates 'invisible' boundaries, across which members of the

Muslim community are not 'welcome' to step. The enactment of both virtual and physical boundaries impacts upon 'emotional geographies' in relation to the way in which Muslims perceive the spaces and places around and outside their communities of abode. Rather than risk the threat of being attacked, either in an online or offline context, many actual and potential victims opt to change their lifestyles and retreat to 'their own' communities.

6
PREVENTION AND RESPONSES

Throughout this study our aim has been victim focused, and as such, the study has been used to empower the people we interviewed by giving them a 'voice' and platform whereby they can make suggestions on what should be done to help prevent Islamophobic hate, both online and offline. In particular, our aim was to bring together those who have experienced Islamophobia to collectively share their views, beliefs and attitudes in terms of what recommendations they perceive as being important to them. Listening to those 'voices' is crucial if we are to make real change and impact with criminal justice agencies, policy makers and other agencies and stakeholders concerned with Islamophobia. The key points that emerge from our findings is that victims would like better protection on public transport, for the police to have a better recording system for Islamophobia, the media to portray a more balanced viewpoint on Muslim communities, and for Islamophobic hostility in the education system to be addressed. We argue that such measures are important and can be incorporated through better awareness of online and offline Islamophobia, providing training for staff on public transport services and for senior editors in the media to be better informed of the key types of Islamophobic abuse that Muslims suffer, both online and offline. Below are the detailed suggestions and recommendations made by the participants with regards to tackling Islamophobia, both online and offline.

1. Islamophobia must be challenged from within Muslim communities

Many of the victims we spoke to felt that Islamophobia is not taken seriously, and recommended that the Muslim community itself be much more confident in recognising, reporting and challenging such incidents. They felt that the community itself could provide help and support to victims of Islamophobia. For example, one of our participants, Hafsa stated that "Change needs to come from within the Muslim community. WE must change this". Other participants expressed similar views, as the following quotes indicate.

'As a convert to Islam it's an eye opener for me but other people, especially Asians, have experienced this every day in their lives; they had to put up with this their entire lives. Some people are too afraid to speak out about it and say "This is unacceptable" because they feel this is the price they have to pay for living in this country. We should not be afraid to stand up and challenge anti-Muslim hate. The community needs to stand up and actually start reporting this and say "Look, this is what our reality looks like, this is what we face". The only way to change things is to stand up for it and challenge people. Until then we will continue to live like this.' (Sarah)

'We need to create awareness and stop blaming the victims. Tell MAMA are doing a great job but we need the different Muslim communities to stand together.' (Safa)

Other participants suggested that raising awareness could be achieved if the community looked for signs from within that might highlight when someone has been targeted and provide support to them. One of the ways this could be achieved could include better resources and educational toolkits placed at mosques and community centres. However, our study did find that for some participants this was not easy, and therefore any sort of work here would require inward thinking and a longer-term solution, such as helping victims improve their levels of confidence in reporting such incidents. For example, highlighting the levels of successful prosecutions and creating better awareness of the support mechanisms for victims would assist in this regard. Furthermore, having the police record Islamophobia as a separate category would also increase levels of confidence amongst victims.

However, one of our participants, Hamza, stated that "If we say anything we are only going to make it worse. That's why we keep quiet". Sadly, the reality is that for most victims of hate crime, reporting it to the police or to other formal agencies can be a barrier. Some of these barriers include shame, embarrassment, fear of retribution, stereotyping from the police and also stigma attached from within communities. Nevertheless, other participants highlighted the importance of reporting Islamophobic incidents to the police, as the following quotes suggest.

'It is important Muslims log everything, and victims and offenders are reported to the appropriate agencies. Logging includes from every bad word to hostile look. If we ignore it, it will only get worse. I also disagree with the victim mentality because it pretends it is not happening. We need to address the situation.' (Kelly)

'We need to make people more aware of these issues, victims must report the abuse.' (Safa)

'People need to speak about this issue and speak up.' (Hira)

However, the majority of victims tend to isolate themselves and suffer in silence. We suggest that Islamophobia resources, packages and a website be designed for Muslim communities to share their stories and also have links to appropriate advice and sources so as to give victims more confidence so that they can report the abuse. We argue this should be more centralised and be available for communities and easy to access both online and offline. This could also include online resources and further links where people can get more information about who to contact if they have suffered this type of abuse in the past.

2. Media training around reporting stories to do with Muslims

Many of the participants noted how Islamophobia and the way in which it is sometimes reported by the media could have an impact on the way people view Muslims and Islam.

'What can we do? We are powerless. We need to find a solution to the Islamophobia we are facing at the moment. It has to be dealt by the media and politicians.' (Ibrahim)

'To be honest with you, it will only get worse, the media will carry on tearing our community apart.' (Ahmed)

'Islamophobia is not going away soon. I'm grateful to Allah that nothing more serious has happened to me. If we fight back, they will make our lives miserable. These people are everywhere, council, police, media, government but they are hidden, they do not show they hate us but they do. They will use all their power to make our lives miserable. People need to learn the truth about Islam and Muslims. Some sections of the media play a massive role in promoting anti-Muslim hate. They always give wrong information about Islam.' (Mohammad)

'We are so demonised that we need to explicitly state that we disagree with the actions of ISIS. Unless we do that, people do not know where we agree or not. Also, a softening approach on the part of the media would help. Channel Four have done a number of programmes during Ramadan to promote positive aspects around Islam, but one thing that does disturb me is when responsible media commentators ask Muslims "How do the ISIS beheadings make you feel?" There is an implicit assumption in that statement that Muslims are responsible and thus need to justify the actions of ISIS, Boko Haram, the murder of Lee Rigby by Adebolajo and Adebowale, and so forth. We should not be held responsible for the actions of people who commit crimes in the name of Islam.' (Adam)

Indeed, we also argue that this can be seen as problematic, in particular when the public may not be aware of what Islam stands for. Allen (2012) found that 64 per cent of the British public claim that they do know about Muslims and what they do know is 'acquired through the media'. In a survey conducted in September 2013 by BBC Radio 1 Newsbeat of 18–24 year-olds, they found that from the 1,000 people questioned, 28 per cent of young people believed Britain would be a safer place with fewer Muslims and 44 per cent of people felt Muslims did not share the same values as the rest of Britain. Interestingly, the people questioned did state that Islamophobia existed in mainstream politics and within the media. They also blamed terrorist groups abroad for this image (26 per cent), and the media was second place at (23 per cent) for depicting Muslims in a negative light, and finally, British Muslims who had committed acts of terrorism were ranked at 21 per cent.

'We need a powerful counter narrative happening and this needs to be supported by politicians and the mass media.' (Sarah)

'The media need to do much more and have an active role in this.' (Fatima)

'We need more balanced reporting from the media. Misinformation about Muslims on the media is a big-big issue.' (Sophie)

'I am a taxi driver, it's always on my mind what customers will think when I pick them up. That's why I try to be an ambassador for Muslims. I explain to customers that what they see in the media is rubbish. But I should not have to do that. I should not need to justify other people's actions.' (Ibrahim)

Particularly striking was a recent news report published by the *Daily Express* on the 10th anniversary of the 7/7 attacks in London, which claimed that there had been an increase in the number of Muslims who 'sympathised' with ISIS. The story appeared to be based on a poll commissioned by the *Daily Mirror* about a possible terrorist attack, and included a survey about people's age, location and social class. However, there was no discussion of religious beliefs. Shortly after, the news story was taken down. Awan and Rahman's (2016) study involved a content analysis of British newspapers and their portrayal of the death of a Muslim pensioner named Mohammed Saleem and the case of Lee Rigby. They found that even though the person convicted of the offence, Pavlo Lapshyn, was arrested and charged for the murder of Mohammed Saleem, a number of British newspapers refused to use the word 'terrorist' to describe the attacker. They stated that:

> Our research suggests that following Woolwich, the print newspaper coverage of Muslim communities in the immediate aftermath provided a lens by which the terms 'Islam and Muslims' were used alongside 'terrorism' in an overtly negative manner. Sadly, we believe that this is a trend within the British press that has often negatively termed Muslims as 'fanatics', 'extremists' and indeed 'terrorists'. We argue that by using the comparison of Mohammed Saleem, who was also a victim of a terrorist attack, a more balanced viewpoint of reporting terrorism is required otherwise we risk as a society stoking up further Islamophobic prejudice as well as exacerbating the potential for unfair treatment of Muslim communities in the country. (Awan and Rahman, 2016: 14)

We believe that training workshops for media professionals with input from the community could help eradicate some of these issues surrounding media stories and bias. These workshops could also include seminars and be conducted by people working with Muslim communities in order to try and better understand the implications of media sensationalism. We also argue that fines could be imposed where stories are reported inaccurately, which aim to demonise and stigmatise Muslim communities.

3. The police can improve the way in which they handle cases of Islamophobia

Our findings suggest that many victims of Islamophobia feel that they are not taken seriously enough by the police and other similar agencies when they report their experiences of Islamophobia. The victims we interviewed spoke about how they had been let down by the police when they reported such incidents. As indicated in the following quote, the way that the police dealt with some participants' cases had impacted upon their perceptions of safety and also whether or not they would report future incidents.

'The police will write the statement but do nothing about it, they are not bothered. They are always late when I call them; they say they have other priorities.' (Mohammad)

'A group of white men came to the halls of residence, shouted Islamophobic comments targeted at me, and urinated on my window. I opened the door, told them I'd phone the police, and they threw a fire extinguisher at my door. When I called the police, they said they didn't have time to come and see me then, so they came the next day. They said they could not find these men because there were no cameras and it was not possible to get DNA from urine. There are double standards, one rule for other communities and one rule for us.' (Aisha)

'If we Muslims get attacked, I do not expect the police to care as much. This is the mentality that exists.' (Bilal)

'The police need to take anti-Muslim hate more seriously. I feel the police don't really care. When I was younger, I had rocks thrown at me and I was actually hit and bruised at the back, and I reported it to the police and they were like "Oh we will go to their house and tell them don't do it again". This experience put me off reporting future incidents.' (Sophie)

When another participant, Safa, reported her experiences to the police of being physically attacked, the response was 'poor' and she felt 'humiliated'. We argue that the police are working to help victims, but in cases where their response is poor, inevitably, this will have an impact on whether victims report incidents because of a lack of confidence and trust in the police. Sarah appreciated these difficulties and stated that "They are understaffed and under resourced and they don't have the capacity to investigate these issues," and Ahmed wanted to see "police officers being trained about Islamophobia. In the same way they set up taskforces to tackle radicalisation and extremism, they need to set up a taskforce to tackle Islamophobia". Clearly, victims of Islamophobia should be treated with respect, empathy and dignity, taking into account their religious and cultural needs (Spalek, 2005). Key agencies, such as the police, are crucial in displaying those characteristics, and through the use of better recording systems such as recording Islamophobia as a separate category, this too can help build confidence and the reporting mechanisms for Islamophobia, both online and offline.

4. The public should intervene and assist victims of Islamophobia on public transport

Many participants spoke about the lack of intervention and assistance from bystanders. As a result, a number of participants told us that they had suffered Islamophobic prejudice, hostility and violence, but people usually remained silent and did not assist victims during or after the ordeal. Crucially, participants spoke about not seeking direct intervention or action but just merely contacting the appropriate services such as the police, which would have benefited them greatly.

> 'I was on the bus and a man shouted to me and my Muslim friends "Oh you are terrorists, I'm gonna come to the back of the bus and stab you". I told the bus driver about this and asked him to stop the bus and call the police but he refused. He said "I am driving the bus, I am just the driver, what do you want me to do about it?"' (Sophie)

Another participant, Hira, was on a train when a group of men began harassing her and dropped alcohol on her coat. However, she insists that the train was full and yet people remained in their seats without offering any sort of assistance or challenging the perpetrator, as demonstrated in the following quote.

> 'People were watching but they ignored it. No one wanted to help.' (Hira)

Such feelings of helplessness can have grave consequences for victims of Islamophobia and can decrease their levels of confidence in reporting future incidents. We argue that tackling Islamophobia should not solely be left to the individual victim but that we as a society must help to tackle this issue when we see it happening in front of our eyes by helping victims and reporting the incident to the police.

5. Islamophobia awareness and visibility

We found that a number of participants were not aware of the term 'Islamophobia', 'online hate crime' and 'hate crime' in general. In particular, amongst those who had experienced online abuse, a number of people were not sure if they had been victims of hate crime. Based on their reports, all the participants had, in fact, suffered hate crime with direct individual threats made against them. Despite this, they were not aware of this or had little if any information on what they should do. Some participants urged the government to raise awareness about this problem.

> 'I don't have confidence in this government that they will do anything about Islamophobia. I think it's totally unfair that the government gave the Jewish community 62 million pounds to protect the community. I don't see the government putting in resources to tackle Islamophobia. We are a larger community than the Jewish community and we are far more vulnerable. It is official that we are ignored. They don't care for us, that is unfair. Theresa May is not a big fan of Muslims. They have not taken Islamophobia seriously. I am not racist, and I am not into anti-Semitism, but the government thinks that the Jewish problem is bigger. This is unfair. I'd like the government to take Islamophobia seriously, that's number one. I'd like them to view Islamophobia as a priority as they do with anti-Semitism. I'd like the government to give us resources to protect our community. I'd like the government to acknowledge that Islamophobia is a problem bigger than the hate crimes that other communities face.' (Ahmed)

When asked what type of awareness participants wanted to see, they stated that they would like to see workshops, advertisements, posters, flyers, reports and other information which they felt should be shared with mosques, community centres, businesses, shops, supermarkets, cafes and schools.

6. Social media companies should make their systems of reporting hate crime more user friendly

As indicated in the following quote, a number of participants spoke about their anger and frustration at reporting online abuse that they had suffered.

> 'Social media companies do not act quickly enough.' (Fatima)

In some cases, the material was removed but reappeared, and in other cases, social media companies refused to take action because the abuse did not breach their specific community standards. We argue that companies such as Twitter and Facebook could use a specific section or button that includes reporting racism, bigotry, hate crime, hate speech and prejudice. The current reporting system around targeted hate should include a contextual analysis of why and how this abuse occurred. A number of participants we spoke to reported being targeted by multiple accounts and that some users had simply changed names or were hiding behind detection. In those cases, participants argued that social media companies had not done enough to track or prevent these users from continuing to use their services.

7. Diversity in the criminal justice system

Our research found that a more inclusive and diverse criminal justice system would allow some victims to feel more confident in reporting incidents of Islamophobia. This was particularly striking when participants discussed the need for Muslim role models and a more diverse criminal justice system.

'It is important to have positive role models and break down people's assumptions and prejudices about Islam. I have a duty to my faith community to continue to wear the hijab and abaya, and be visibly identifiable as a Muslim.' (Sarah)

'It will take generations before anything changes. Terrorism goes hand in hand with being a Muslim in people's minds. Change needs to come from the West. Rather than explaining Islamic culture, defending Islam and trying to change mindsets, we need to stop apologising for Islam, stop explaining, stop defending Islam. We must not play their games. We're losing when we are responding to every accusation we get. What we need to do is build ourselves. Strengthen up, build internally, be role models, be more successful.' (Bilal)

'Islamophobia exists in the superclass, the judges, the government, the police and they can get away with it. We don't have Asians or Muslims in these jobs and this is dangerous I believe.' (Ibrahim)

We argue that agencies such as victim support, the police, the judiciary and other key stakeholders should have a more diverse and representative sample from within communities such as the wider Muslim communities.

8. Challenging Islamophobic rhetoric and engaging schools in the debate

We argue that the language around Islamophobic hate should be challenged within schools as a means to help young people better understand the consequences of this form of hate crime. For example, this could be done through the use of posters that both highlight specific terms and create awareness amongst children and young people that Islamophobia is not 'cool'. We strongly argue that this could be done through workshops, graffiti classroom based lessons, in assemblies and in the classroom with activities and rewards for people who are able to engage with this debate in an open and safe space. We feel a marketing campaign here such as: 'I am a Muslim, I may wear a headscarf or have a beard, but I am British and proud of it' could be used as a vehicle to break down barriers.

Concluding thoughts

The preceding discussion throughout the book has been about the findings of our study regarding the online and offline experiences of Islamophobia amongst Muslim men and women in the UK. Specifically, the aim of this study was to examine: (a) the nature and extent of online and offline Islamophobia directed towards Muslims in the UK; (b) the impact of this hostility upon victims, their families and wider Muslim communities; (c) offer recommendations on preventing and responding to Islamophobic hate crime. The study included 20 in-depth interviews with Muslims who have been victims of online and offline Islamophobic hate crime, and had reported these experiences to Tell MAMA.

Key themes that emerged from the research findings included the triggers of Islamophobic hate crime, the nature and extent of online and offline Islamophobic abuse, and the consequences for victims, their families and wider Muslim communities. Iganski (2001: 636) argues that 'There is an emerging consensus in the literature that little is known about the effects of hate crimes beyond the impact on the initial victims. Even the effects on the initial victims are under researched'. We found that the prevalence and severity of online and offline Islamophobic hate crimes are influenced by 'trigger' events of local, national and international significance (Williams and Tregidga, 2014). Terrorist attacks carried out by individuals who identify themselves as being Muslim or acting in the name of Islam – such as the Woolwich attack, the atrocities committed by ISIS and attacks around the world, such as in Sydney, Paris, Copenhagen and Tunisia – induced a significant increase in participants' experiences of online and offline Islamophobia. Additionally, national scandals such as the child sexual exploitation in Rotherham by groups of Pakistani men, and the alleged 'Trojan Horse' scandal in Birmingham framed as a 'jihadist plot' to take over schools, were also highlighted by participants as 'trigger' events, which increased their vulnerability to Islamophobic hostility, both online and offline.

Participants reported suffering Islamophobic hostility on a daily basis, ranging from online threats and messages of hate to harassment, intimidation and violence in the 'real' world. They highlighted that the visibility of their Muslim identity was key to being identified as Muslims, and thus triggering online and/or offline Islamophobic attacks. Female participants felt more vulnerable to this victimisation in comparison to male participants, both online and offline. As might be expected, both online and offline Islamophobia increased feelings of vulnerability, fear and insecurity amongst participants (Qureshi, 2012). They also suffered a range of psychological and emotional responses such as low confidence, depression and anxiety. Throughout interviews, participants highlighted the relationship between online and offline Islamophobic hate crimes, and described living in fear because of the possibility of online threats materialising in the 'real' world. The constant threat of Islamophobic hate had forced participants to adopt a siege mentality and keep a low profile in order to reduce the potential for future attacks. Many participants reported taking steps to become less 'visible', for example by taking the headscarf off for women, and shaving their beards for men (Rowe, 2004; Smith, et al, 2012).

We asked participants what they felt should be done to prevent Islamophobic hate crime, both online and offline. They made a number of recommendations including encouraging fellow Muslims and wider Muslim communities to be confident in recognising, reporting and challenging such incidents; better media training in order to report stories about Muslims and Islam fairly without stereotyping them as 'terrorists', 'extremists' and 'radicals'; the police taking steps to increase the confidence of victims; witnesses intervening (where possible and safe) to protect, assist victims of Islamophobia and inform the police; more information in the form of workshops, advertisements, posters, flyers, reports promoted in mosques, community centres, businesses, shops, cafes and schools; social media companies making their systems of reporting hate crime more user friendly; diversity in the criminal justice system; challenging Islamophobic rhetoric and engaging schools in the debate. This also includes the police recording Islamophobic hate crime as a separate category and making public transport safer.

We hope that through this study we have raised awareness of both online and offline Islamophobia and that these recommendations can be used by policy makers, community organisations, charities and the police to better understand the challenges, causes and consequences for victims of Islamophobic hostility, violence and abuse. These recommendations are important because they provide the context behind which victims feel they could have an improved service and system whereby confidence can be restored within the criminal justice system. Therefore, for the participants we spoke to, they appreciated the challenges the police and other agencies faced when confronting Islamophobic hate crime but felt a strong passion and desire for things to be improved, and throughout their experiences stayed resolute in their will and desire for real change at both a policy and grassroots level.

References

Allen, C. (2010) *Islamophobia*, Surrey: Ashgate.

Allen, C. (2012) *A review of the evidence relating to the representation of Muslims and Islam in the British media,* Birmingham: University of Birmingham.

Allen, C., Isakjee, A. and Young, O. (2013) *Understanding the impact of anti-Muslim hate on Muslim women*, Birmingham: University of Birmingham.

Allen, C. and Nielsen, J. (2002) *Summary report on Islamophobia in the EU after 11 September 2001*, Vienna: European Monitoring Centre on Racism and Xenophobia.

Allport, G.W. (1954) *The nature of prejudice*, Reading, MA: Addison-Wesley.

Awan, I. (2012) 'The impact of policing British Muslims: A qualitative exploration', *Journal of Policing, Intelligence and Counter-Terrorism*, 7(1): 22-35.

Awan, I. (2014) 'Islamophobia on Twitter: A typology of online hate against Muslims on social media', *Policy & Internet*, 6(2): 133-50.

Awan, I. (2016) (ed) *Islamophobia in cyberspace: Hate crimes go viral*, New York: Routledge.

Awan, I. and Blakemore, B. (2012) *Policing cyber hate, cyber threats and cyber terrorism*, Farnham: Ashgate.

Awan, I. and Rahman, M. (2016) 'Portrayal of Muslims following the murders of Lee Rigby in Woolwich and Mohammed Saleem in Birmingham: A content analysis of UK newspapers', *Journal of Muslim Minority Affairs,* (Early Access) DOI: 10.1080/13602004.2016.1147151.

BBC News (2015) *Police seek talks following Rotherham Muslim boycott,* [online] Available at: http://www.bbc.co.uk/news/uk-england-south-yorkshire-34637505 [accessed July 2016].

Berg, B.L. (2007) 'A dramaturgical look at interviewing', in B.L. Berg and H. Lune (eds) *Qualitative research methods for the social sciences* (6th edn), Boston: Allyn & Bacon, pp 89-143.

Bowling, B. (2009) 'Violent racism: Victimisation, policing and social context', in B. Williams and H. Goodman-Chong (eds) *Victims and victimisation: A reader,* Maidenhead: Open University Press, pp 45-57.

Brown, M.D. (2001) 'Multiple meanings of the hijab in contemporary France', in W.J.F. Keenan (ed) *Dressed to impress: Looking the part,* Oxford: Berg, pp 105-21.

Bryman, A. (2008) *Social research methods* (4th edn), New York: Oxford University Press.

Chan, J.B.L. (2007) 'Police and new technologies', in T. Newburn (ed) *Handbook of policing,* Cullompton: Willan Publishing, pp 655-79.

Chakraborti, N. and Garland, J. (2009) *Hate crime: Impact, causes and responses,* London: Sage.

Chakraborti, N., Garland, J. and Hardy, S. (2014) *The hate crime project,* Leicester: University of Leicester.

Charmaz, K. (2006) *Constructing grounded theory: A practice guide through qualitative analysis,* London: Sage.

Cole, J. and Cole, B. (2009) *Martyrdom: Radicalisation and terrorist Vviolence among British Muslims,* London: Pennant Books.

Cole, M. and Maisuria, A. (2007) 'Shut the f*** up', 'you have no rights here': Critical race theory and racialisation in post-7/7 racist Britain, *Journal for Critical Education Policy Studies,* 5(1): 1-27.

Coliandris, G. (2012) 'Hate in a cyber age', in I. Awan and B. Blakemore (eds) *Policing cyber hate, cyber threats and cyber terrorism,* Farnham: Ashgate, pp 75-95.

College of Policing (2014) *Hate crime operational guidance*, [online] Available at: http://www.report-it.org.uk/files/hate_crime_operational_guidance.pdf [accessed July 2016].

Collins, P.H. (2000) *Black feminist thought: Knowledge, consciousness and the politics of empowerment*, London: Routledge.

Commission on British Muslims and Islamophobia (2004) *Islamophobia: Issues, challenges and action*, Stoke on Trent: Trentham Books.

Craig, K. (2002) 'Examining Hate-motivated Aggression: A Review of the Social Psychological Literature on Hate Crime as a Distinct Form of Aggression', *Aggression and Violent Behaviour*, 7(1): 85-101.

Crenshaw, K. (1991) 'Mapping the margins: Intersectionality, identity politics and violence against women of color', *Stanford Law Review* 43(6): 1241-99.

Crown Prosecution Service (2013) *Guidelines on prosecuting cases involving communications sent via social media*, [online] Available at: http://www.cps.gov.uk/legal/a_to_c/communications_sent_via_social_media/ [accessed July 2016].

Curtis, B. and Curtis, C. (2011) *Social research*, London: Sage.

Denzin, N.K. and Lincoln, Y.S. (2008) *Handbook of qualitative research* (2nd edn), Thousand Oaks, CA: Sage.

Dodd, V. and Williams, M. (2014) *British Muslims fear backlash after David Haines murder*, [online] Available at: http://www.theguardian.com/world/2014/sep/14/britain-muslims-backlash-fear-david-haines-murder [accessed July 2016].

Feldman, M., Littler, M., Dack, J. and Copsey, N. (2013) *Anti-Muslim hate crime and the far right*, Middlesbrough: Teesside University.

Finlay, L. (2002) 'Negotiating the swamp: the opportunity and challenge of reflexivity in research practice', *Qualitative Research*, 2(2): 209-230.

Forum Against Islamophobia and Racism (2013) *Islamophobia*, [online] Available at: http://www.fairuk.org [accessed July 2016].

Garland, J. and Chakraborti, N. (2012) 'Divided by a common concept? Assessing the implications of different conceptualizations of hate crime in the European Union', *European Journal of Criminology*, 9(1): 38-51.

Gerstenfeld, P.B. (2013) *Hate crimes: Causes, controls and controversies* (3rd edn), Thousand Oaks, CA: Sage.

Githens-Mazer, J. and Lambert, R. (2010) *Islamophobia and anti-Muslim hate crime: A London case study*, London: European Muslim Research Centre.

Glaser, B.G. (1992) *Emergence vs forcing: Basics of grounded theory analysis*, Mill Valley, CA: Sociology Press.

Glaser, B.G. and Strauss, A. (1967) *The discovery of grounded theory*, New York: Academic Press.

Green, J. and Thorogood, N. (2004) *Qualitative methods for health research*, London: Sage.

Hall, N. (2013) *Hate crime* (2nd edn), London: Routledge.

Hammersley, M. and Atkinson, P. (1983) *Ethnography: principles in practice*, London: Tavistock.

Hanes, E. and Machin, S. (2014) 'Hate crime in the wake of terror attacks: Evidence from 7/7 and 9/11', *Journal of Contemporary Criminal Justice,* 30: 247-67.

Hayfield, N. and Huxley, C. (2015) 'Insider and outsider perspectives: Reflections on researcher identities in research with lesbian and bisexual women', *Qualitative Research in Psychology* 12(2): 91-106.

Hennink, M., Hutter, I. and Bailey, A. (2011) *Qualitative research methods*, London: Sage.

Herek, G., Cogan, J. and Gillis, R. (2002) 'Victim experiences in hate crimes based on sexual orientation,' *Journal of Social Issues,* 58 (2): 319-39.

Hesse-Biber, S. and Leavy, P. (2006) *The practice of qualitative research*, Thousand Oaks: Sage.

The Huffington Post (2013) *Twitter rape abuse of Caroline Criado-Perez leads to boycott threat*, [online] Available at: http://www.huffingtonpost.co.uk/2013/07/27/twitter-rape-abuse_n_3663904.html [accessed July 2016].

Huntington, S. (1996) T*he clash of civilizations and the remaking of world order*, New York, NY: Simon and Schuster.

Iganski, P. (2001) 'Hate crimes hurt more,' *American Behavioural Scientist,* 45(4): 626-38.

REFERENCES

Kanuha, V.K. (2000) '"Being" native versus "going native": Conducting social work research as an insider', *Social Work*, 45(5): 439-47.

Keats, D. (2014) *Hate crimes in cyberspace*, Cambridge, MA: Harvard University Press.

King, R.D. and Sutton, G.M. (2014) 'High times for hate crimes: Explaining the temporal clustering of hate motivated offending', *Criminology*, 51: 871-94.

Kotecha, S. (2013) 'Quarter of young British people "do not trust Muslims"', *BBC Newsbeat*, [online] Available at: http://www.bbc.co.uk/newsbeat/24204742 [accessed July 2016].

Labaree, R.V. (2002) "The risk of 'going observationalist': negotiating the hidden dilemmas of being an insider participant observer", *Qualitative Research* 2(1): 97-122.

Lancashire Telegraph (2014) *Spike in anti-Muslim abuse by children after Lee Rigby murder*, [online] Available at: http://www.lancashiretelegraph.co.uk/news/11309996.Spike_in_anti_muslim_abuse_by_children_after_Lee_Rigby_murder/ [accessed July 2016].

Lazenby, P. (2013) *Attacks on Muslims soar to make 2013 the year of hate*, [online] Available at: http://www.morningstaronline.co.uk/a-243c-Attacks-on-muslims-soar-to-make-2013-the-year-of-hate#.Vx6F3WPAdsM [accessed July 2016].

Littler, M. and Feldman, M. (2015) *Tell MAMA reporting 2014/2015: Annual monitoring, cumulative extremism, and policy implications*, Teesside: Teesside University Press.

Mason, J. (2002) *Qualitative researching*, London: Sage.

Maxfield, M.G. and Babbie, E.R. (2009) *Basics of research methods for criminal justice and criminology* (3nd edn), Belmont: Thompson.

McDevitt, J., Balboni, J., Garcia, L. and Gu, J. (2001) 'Consequences for victims: A comparison of bias- and non-bias-motivated assaults', *American Behavioral Scientist*, 45(4): 697-713.

McGhee, D. (2005) *Intolerant Britain? Hate, citizenship and difference*, Milton Keynes: Open University Press.

McKenna, K. and Bargh, J. (1998) 'Coming out in the age of the internet: Identity demarginalization through virtual group participation', *Journal of Personality and Social Psychology*, 75: 681-94.

Meer, N., Dwyer, C. and Modood, T. (2010) 'Embodying Nationhood? Conceptions of British national identity, citizenship and gender in the "Veil Affair"', *The Sociological Review*, 58(1): 84-111.

Modood, T. (2003) 'Muslims and European multiculturalism', in S. Spencer (ed) *The politics of migration: Managing opportunity, conflict and chance*, Oxford: Blackwell Publishing, pp 100-15.

Mythen, G., Walklate, S. and Khan, F. (2009) '"I'm a Muslim, but I'm not a Terrorist": Victimization, risky identities and the performance of safety', British Journal of Criminology, 49(6): 736-54.

Otis, M.D. and W.F. Skinner (1996) 'The prevalence of victimization and its effect on mental well-being among lesbian and gay people', *Journal of Homosexuality*, 30(3): 93-121.

Padela, A. and Heisler, M. (2010) 'The association of perceived abuse and discrimination after September 11, 2001, with psychological distress, level of happiness, and health status among Arab Americans', *American Journal of Public Health*, 100(2): 284-91.

Payne, S. (2004) 'Designing and conducting qualitative studies', in S. Michie and C. Abraham (eds) *Health psychology in practice*, London: Routledge, pp 126-49.

Perry, B. (2001) *In the name of hate: Understanding hate crimes*, London: Routledge.

Perry, B. (2003) 'Where do we go from here? Researching hate crime', *Internet Journal of Criminology*, [online] Available at: http://www.internetjournalofcriminology.com/where%20do%20we%20go%20from%20here.%20researching%20hate%20crime.pdf [accessed July 2016].

Perry, B. and Alvi, S. (2012) '"We are all vulnerable": The in terrorem effects of hate crimes', *International Review of Victimology*, 18: 57-71.

Perry, B. and Olsson, P. (2009) 'Cyberhate: The globalisation of hate', *Information & Communications Technology Law*, 18(2): 185-99.

Pillow, W. (2003) 'Confession, catharsis, or cure? Rethinking the uses of reflexivity as methodological power in qualitative research', *Qualitative Studies in Education*, 16: 175-96.

Prince, J. (2012) 'Psychological aspects of cyber hate and cyber terrorism', in I. Awan and B. Blakemore (eds) *Policing cyber hate, cyber threats and cyber terrorism*, Farnham: Ashgate, pp 39-55.

Qureshi, H. (2012) 'Online racist abuse: We've all suffered it', *The Guardian*, [online] Available at: http://www.theguardian.com/commentisfree/2012/jul/11/online-racist-abuse-writers-face [accessed July 2016].

Rowe, M. (2004). *Policing, race and racism*, Cullompton: Willan Publishing.

The Runnymede Trust (1997) *Islamophobia a challenge for us all*, [online] Available at: http://www.runnymedetrust.org/uploads/publications/pdfs/islamophobia.pdf [accessed July 2016].

Sallah, M. (2010) *The Ummah and Ethnicity: Listening to the Voices of African Heritage Muslims in Leicester*, Leicester: Leicester City Council.

Savvides N., Al-Youssef J., Colin, M. and Garrido, C. (2014) 'Journeys into inner/outer space: Reflections on the methodological challenges of negotiating insider/outsider status in international educational research', *Research in Comparative and International Education*, 9(4): 412-25.

Shah, S. (2004) 'The researcher/interviewer in intercultural context: A social intruder!' *British Educational Research Journal*, 30(4): 549-75.

Sheridan, L. (2006) 'Islamophobia pre-and post-September 11th 2001', *Journal of Interpersonal Violence*, 21(3): 317-36.

Silverman, D. (2013) *Doing qualitative research* (4th edn), London: Sage.

Smith, K., Lader, D., Hoare, J. and Lau, I. (2012) *Hate crime, cyber security and the experience of crime among children: Findings from the 2010/11 British Crime Survey*, London: Home Office.

Spalek, B. (2005) 'A critical reflection on researching black Muslim women's lives post-September 11th', *International Journal of Social Research Methodology*, 8(5): 405-18.

Spiers, J. (2000) 'New perspectives on vulnerability using emic and etic approaches', *Journal of Advanced Nursing*, 31(3): 715-21.

Tajfel, H. (1970) 'Experiments in intergroup discrimination', *Scientific American*, 223: 96-102.

Taras, R. (2012) *Xenophobia and Islamophobia in Europe*, Edinburgh: University Press.

Urquhart, C. (2013) 'Attacks on Muslims soar in wake of Woolwich murder', *The Guardian*, [online] Available at: http://www.theguardian.com/uk/2013/may/25/woolwich-murder-attacks-on-muslims [accessed July 2016].

Watt, P. (2014) 'Nick Clegg: Birmingham schools row coverage may have raised Islamophobia', *The Guardian*, [online] Available at: http://www.theguardian.com/politics/2014/jun/20/nick-clegg-birmingham-schools-islamophobia [accessed July 2016].

Weller, P., Feldman, A. and Purdam, K. (2001) *Religious discrimination in England and Wales: Home Office research report 220,* London: Home Office.

Williams, M.L. and Burnap, P. (2015) 'Cyberhate on social media in the aftermath of Woolwich: A case study in computational criminology and big data', *British Journal of Criminology*, 55(5): 944-65.

Williams, M. and Tregidga, J. (2014) 'Hate crime victimisation in Wales: Psychological and physical impacts across seven hate crime victim-types', *British Journal of Criminology*, 54(4): 946-67.

Yar, M. (2013) *Cybercrime and society*, London: Sage.

Yuval-Davis, N. (2011) *The politics of belonging: Intersectional contestations*, London: Sage.

Zempi, I. (2014) *Uncovering Islamophobia: The victimisation of veiled Muslim women*, Leicester: University of Leicester.

Index